D1320958

4.2008

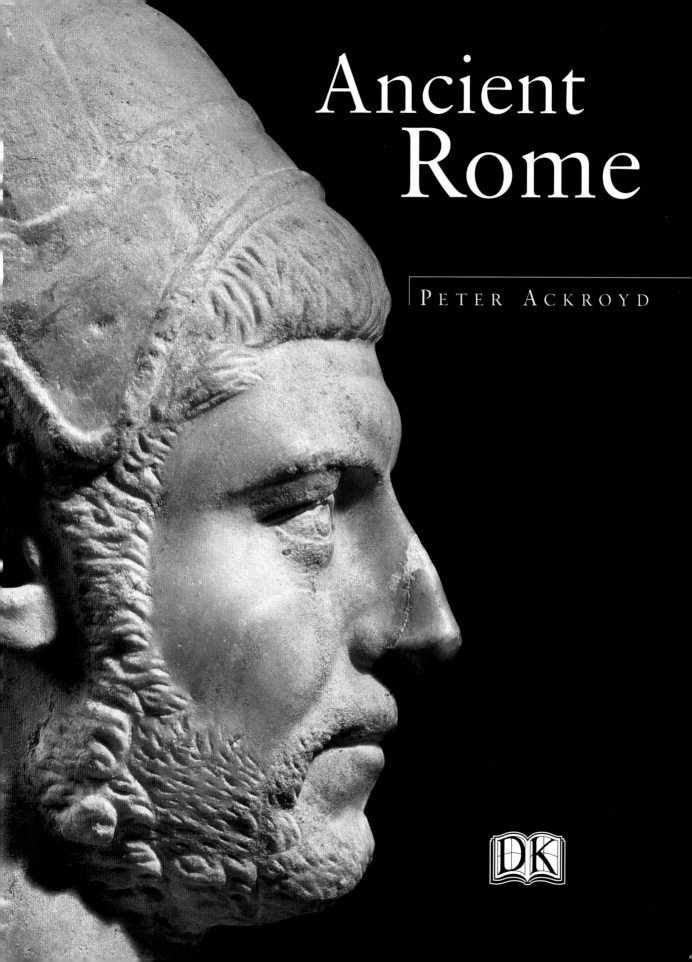

Ancient
Rome

PETER ACKROYD

DK

LONDON, NEW YORK, MUNICH,
MELBOURNE, and DELHI

Project editor Hazel Beynon
Editor Susan Kennedy
Designer Shefali Upadhyay
Managing art editor Diane Thistlethwaite
Senior editor David John
Managing editor Linda Esposito
Publishing managers Caroline Buckingham,
Andrew Macintyre
Art director Simon Webb
Publishing director Jonathan Metcalf
Production controller Luca Bazzoli
DTP designer Siu Yin Ho
DK Cartography Paul Eames
Picture researcher Sarah Hopper
Picture librarians Rose Horridge, Kate
Ledwith, Sarah Mills
Jacket designer Neal Cobourne

Consultant
Professor Peter Salway

First published in Great Britain in 2005 by
Dorling Kindersley Limited
80 Strand, London WC2R 0RL

A Penguin Company

2 4 6 8 10 9 7 5 3 1

Copyright © 2005 Dorling Kindersley Limited
Text copyright © 2005 Peter Ackroyd

All rights reserved. No part of this publication may be
reproduced, stored in a retrieval system, or transmitted
in any form or by any means, electronic, mechanical,
photocopying, recording or otherwise, without the
prior written permission of the copyright owner.

A CIP catalogue record for this book is
available from the British Library.

ISBN 1 4053 0734 X

Reproduced by Colourscan
Printed and bound in China by Hung Hing

See our complete catalogue at
www.dk.com

Contents

This is the **story** of how a group of villages became a city, and how that city became the greatest world **power** of its age.

From a small city ruled by kings, Rome became a republic that elected its own leaders and finally an imperial capital that dominated most of the known world – a feat unsurpassed since the time of Alexander the Great. The story of Rome is the story of ambition that led to power and greatness. Over time, that greatness was weakened by the Romans' love of wealth and luxury. The city of Rome began strong and healthy, but declined with age and prosperity. Its first citizens were hardworking farmers and soldiers, but by the time of the empire, many had become pampered and lazy.

The city of Rome first made itself master of Italy. It went on to conquer a vast empire that stretched around the Mediterranean Sea and included countries as distant and diverse as Britain and

UNIVERSITY OF CHICHESTER

Asia Minor (modern Turkey). It extended from Portugal in the west to Syria in the east, from the lowlands of Scotland in the north to Egypt in the south. It brought together what are now at least 30 separate countries in Europe, the Middle East and North Africa. It unified Europe in ways that have not been achieved since – even in the 21st century – by determining that one official language and one currency would be used throughout this vast area. The Romans taught the world the virtues of religious tolerance as well as the advantages of town living. They also taught the citizens of its empire the merits of peace and order. It may have been an order maintained by military force, but we shall see that it brought many benefits.

The Roman empire crumbled more than 1,500 years ago, but its legacy is still with us. Many of its great roads and monuments survive. Latin, the language of the Romans, is still taught throughout the world. The writers and orators of the Roman Republic inspired the later leaders of the French Revolution and the American Revolution. The example of the Roman empire was a mighty force in the establishment of the British empire. So this is the story of how the Romans helped to form the world as we know it.

CHAPTER ONE

The time of the kings

From a small settlement on the banks of the River Tiber in Italy, Rome grew into one of largest and most powerful empires the world had ever seen. At the heart of the empire, lay the city of Rome – one of the most splendid cities of the ancient world.

THE CITY OF ROME WAS built on seven hills, the most important of which were the Palatine Hill and the Capitoline Hill. The site of the city was by a ford, or crossing place, on the River Tiber. It was an ideal location for a city. The area was fertile and surrounded by hills, and the Tiber provided an important route for trade and communication.

Before Rome's rise to power, the land of Italy was occupied by a variety of tribes, such as the Sabines and the Samnites. The region around Rome was called Latium and was inhabited by a tribe of people known as the Latins. These people were herders and farmers, who lived in a group of small villages on the hills around Rome. The south of Italy was dominated by the Greeks, who had set up colonies there as early as 750 BCE. To the north lay Etruria, the home of an

◀ An Etruscan wine-bearer at a banquet

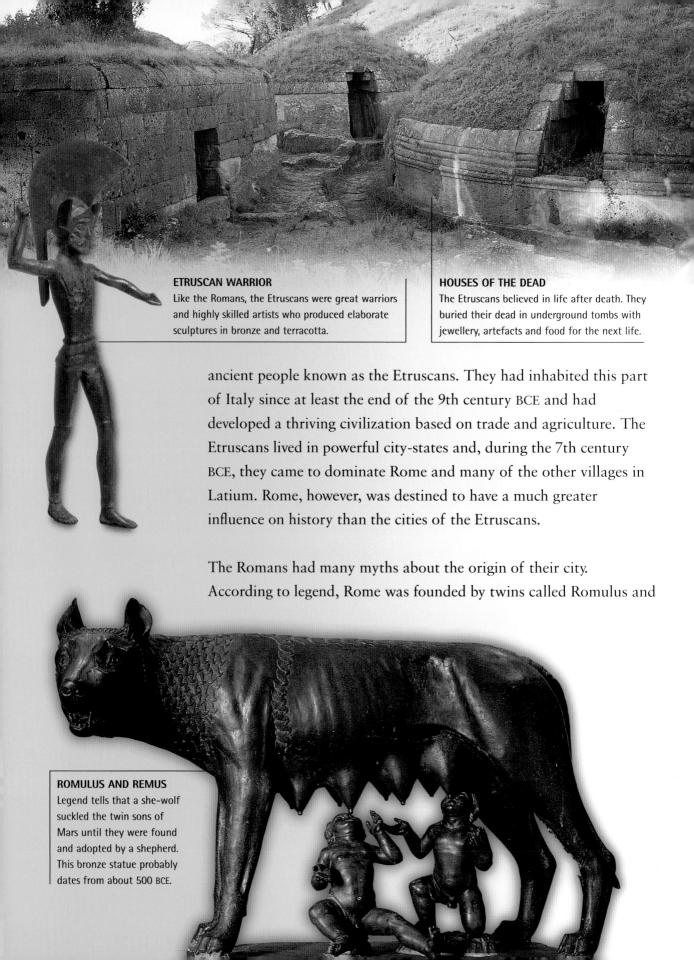

ETRUSCAN WARRIOR
Like the Romans, the Etruscans were great warriors and highly skilled artists who produced elaborate sculptures in bronze and terracotta.

HOUSES OF THE DEAD
The Etruscans believed in life after death. They buried their dead in underground tombs with jewellery, artefacts and food for the next life.

ancient people known as the Etruscans. They had inhabited this part of Italy since at least the end of the 9th century BCE and had developed a thriving civilization based on trade and agriculture. The Etruscans lived in powerful city-states and, during the 7th century BCE, they came to dominate Rome and many of the other villages in Latium. Rome, however, was destined to have a much greater influence on history than the cities of the Etruscans.

The Romans had many myths about the origin of their city. According to legend, Rome was founded by twins called Romulus and

ROMULUS AND REMUS
Legend tells that a she-wolf suckled the twin sons of Mars until they were found and adopted by a shepherd. This bronze statue probably dates from about 500 BCE.

Remus. The twins were said to be the sons of Mars, the god of war. Their mother was Ilia, the daughter of King Numitor. Before the boys were born, Numitor had been ousted from the throne by his brother, Amulius. When Ilia gave birth to the twins, Amulius feared a threat to his power and ordered the boys to be drowned in the Tiber. Instead, they were left in the forest to be eaten by wild beasts. Against all odds they survived. When Romulus and Remus grew up, they decided to build a new city in the hilly woods of Latium. But they disagreed over the boundaries of that city and, during a violent argument, Romulus killed Remus with a blow to the head. Romulus became the first king of the new city, which bore his name.

In later times, when Rome had risen to become the greatest power in the world, the Romans came to believe that their city had always been destined for greatness, and historians began to record its past. In 29 BCE, a historian named Livy collected together the myths and legends of early Rome that had been handed down through the ages. According to Livy, the birthdate of Rome was 21st April 753 BCE. Interestingly, this may be quite close to the actual date when the city was founded. It seems that, in the course of the 7th century BCE, a number of villages that had grown up around the seven hills came together and formed one settlement. Over time, the simple wooden huts of the early inhabitants gave way to more permanent brick buildings that stood within a defensive wall and a sacred boundary known as the *pomerium*. By the end of the 6th century BCE, larger public and private buildings had been erected, and the marshes within the city walls had been drained to provide better land.

It is generally agreed that the first rulers of Rome were kings. History books usually say there were seven kings, but that may just be a convenient number relating to the seven hills of Rome.

WALLED TOWN
This medieval painting shows the small town of Viterbo, which lies on the site of an ancient Etruscan settlement in the Latium region. The early city of Rome would have looked similar to this walled town.

CROWNING GLORY
The Romans came to despise the memory of the early kings, and no royal portraits have survived. As a symbol of their power, kings wore a decorated headband called a diadem, similar to the one worn by this Egyptian priest.

The king was in charge of the religious ceremonies of the city. He made war and peace with other cities in the region and he decided the law. He wore a purple toga or cloak and rode in an ivory chariot. He was attended by servants who carried a symbol of his authority called the *fasces* (a bundle of rods tied to an axe with a red strap).

LASTING SYMBOL
The *fasces* later became the symbol of Rome itself. This badge carries the initials *SPQR*, which stand for "the Senate and People of Rome".

During the time of the kings, the city was improved and beautified. In the centre of Rome, the area known as the Forum was paved, and public buildings and temples were built around it. A great temple dedicated to Jupiter was erected on the Capitoline Hill. Jupiter, the sky-god, was to become the chief god of the Roman state, and his shrine on the Capitol would become the city's most sacred site.

TEMPLE OF JUPITER
The Romans called the god Jupiter *Optimus Maximus*, which means "the Greatest and Best". This painting shows his temple (below left) in the 2nd century BCE.

The kings ruled over Rome for more than 200 years. They were chosen and advised by an influential body of *senes* (elders), who were all members of Rome's wealthy and aristocratic families. These families became known as the *patricii* or patricians. Everyone who was not a patrician was classed as a plebeian or pleb. This division in society would have profound effects for the whole history of Rome.

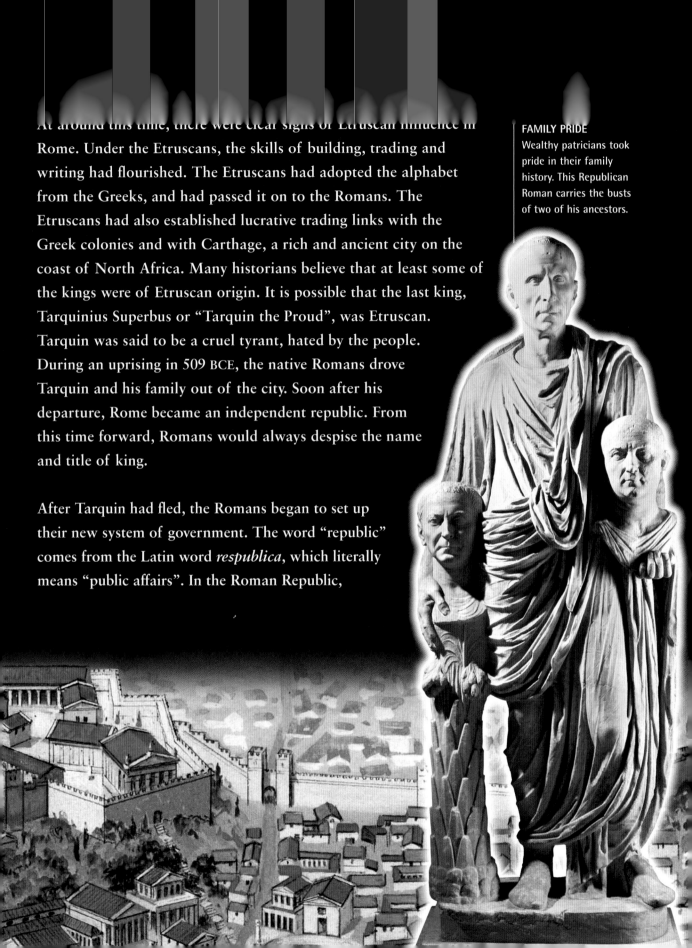

At around this time, there were clear signs of Etruscan influence in Rome. Under the Etruscans, the skills of building, trading and writing had flourished. The Etruscans had adopted the alphabet from the Greeks, and had passed it on to the Romans. The Etruscans had also established lucrative trading links with the Greek colonies and with Carthage, a rich and ancient city on the coast of North Africa. Many historians believe that at least some of the kings were of Etruscan origin. It is possible that the last king, Tarquinius Superbus or "Tarquin the Proud", was Etruscan. Tarquin was said to be a cruel tyrant, hated by the people. During an uprising in 509 BCE, the native Romans drove Tarquin and his family out of the city. Soon after his departure, Rome became an independent republic. From this time forward, Romans would always despise the name and title of king.

After Tarquin had fled, the Romans began to set up their new system of government. The word "republic" comes from the Latin word *respublica*, which literally means "public affairs". In the Roman Republic,

FAMILY PRIDE
Wealthy patricians took pride in their family history. This Republican Roman carries the busts of two of his ancestors.

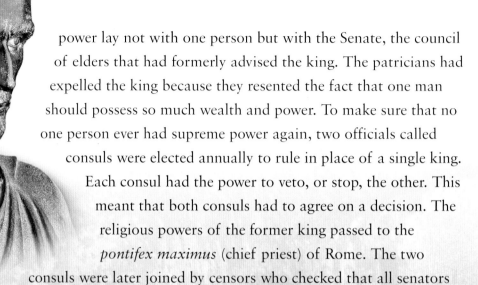

power lay not with one person but with the Senate, the council of elders that had formerly advised the king. The patricians had expelled the king because they resented the fact that one man should possess so much wealth and power. To make sure that no one person ever had supreme power again, two officials called consuls were elected annually to rule in place of a single king. Each consul had the power to veto, or stop, the other. This meant that both consuls had to agree on a decision. The religious powers of the former king passed to the *pontifex maximus* (chief priest) of Rome. The two consuls were later joined by censors who checked that all senators were genuine Roman citizens. In Roman society, everyone was classed as either a citizen or non-citizen. Citizens had to be born in Rome and had special rights (such as the right to vote). Non-citizens were either slaves or provincials (people who lived outside Rome).

A FOUNDING FATHER
Every year Roman citizens elected senators to be government officials. This bronze head is thought to represent Brutus, a founding father of the Republic.

The plebeians, or ordinary people of Rome, had not been responsible for the removal of the kings and often resented the authority of the patricians. In 494 BCE, the plebeians rebelled and refused to serve in the army. Their refusal was a serious matter for a city that needed strong defences. The patricians were therefore forced to agree to the annual election of two representatives of the people, known as tribunes, to protect the interests of the plebeians against the consuls and the patricians. In later times, the number of tribunes was increased from two to ten.

ADDRESSING THE SENATE
In the early days of the Republic, only patricians were allowed to attend the *curia*, or Senate house.

Governing Rome

The Senate managed the city's affairs and was made up of officials elected by the assemblies. Senators were chosen from Rome's wealthiest and most powerful families. Elected from the Senate were consuls, *quaestors*, *aediles*, *praetors*, and religious officials. There were also censors, who revised Senate membership and issued contracts for temples and roads.

Quaestors *were in charge of Rome's finances.*

Praetors *were in charge of justice.*

Aediles *were responsible for the upkeep of the city.*

Tribunes were elected by the people.

The two consuls were elected for a year at a time.

THE PEOPLE OF ROME
Plebeian farmers, artisans and shopkeepers made up the mass of Roman citizens. Wealthy plebeians, such as bankers or merchants, were known as *equites*.

There was also a plebeian assembly, but at the beginning, it did not possess much political power. The plebeians as a whole, however, did have a certain amount of power over their own destinies. If they refused to serve in the army, then the Republic could not be defended. It was as simple as that. So, it was always considered important that the patricians and plebeians worked together for the sake of the entire city. That was one of the early strengths of Rome.

In approximately 450 BCE, after a series of riots by the plebeians, the magistrates drew up a written set of laws called the Twelve Tables. A copy of these laws was displayed in the Forum in the centre of the city. There were laws covering all aspects of Roman life. There were laws about the penalties for murder and for accidental killing. There were also laws about marriages and about debts. The publication of the Twelve Tables was an early sign that the Romans took their legal system very seriously indeed. Their code of laws, once established throughout the empire, would provide a model for the rest of Europe for many centuries.

Almost as soon as Rome had become a republic, it began to test its strength in a series of wars against its neighbours. It seems to have been a city born for warfare and conquest. There was also an increasing need for land. The population of the city had begun to rise so rapidly that Rome was becoming overcrowded. By taking over large areas of territory and setting up new towns called colonies, the Romans set about extending their empire. Throughout the 5th and 4th centuries BCE, Rome waged war against nearby lands. Naturally, its

OFFICER OF THE LAW
Officials called *lictors* escorted important Roman officials, such as magistrates, and carried the *fasces* as a sign of office.

NEW TERRITORY
With an increasing population, Rome needed more land. It conquered neighbouring towns before moving further afield.

neighbours attacked back. Fierce tribes, such as the Volsci, the Aequi and the Sabines, continually raided inside Roman territory and, on some occasions, came perilously close to the city itself. In addition to these tribes, the Romans fought a long war against the Etruscans of the nearby city of Veii, north of Rome. Veii was a prosperous city with much fertile territory at its disposal. It fought off several Roman attempts to conquer it before the city finally surrendered in 396 BCE.

But six years later, a Celtic-speaking tribe, known to the Romans as Gauls, attacked Rome at night and devastated the city. Only a small group of soldiers on the Capitoline Hill survived. According to legend, the soldiers were woken up by the cackling and flapping of the holy geese kept within the sacred enclosure. But the invading tribesmen sacked the rest of the city and besieged the Capitol for seven months. The Gauls left only after they were paid a large sum of gold as booty.

STOLEN WOMEN
Legend relates that, due to a shortage of women in the city, the Romans attacked the Sabines and kidnapped their wives and daughters.

SACRED GEESE
The geese on the Capitoline Hill were sacred to the goddess Juno. The historian Livy records how their cackling saved Rome.

CELTIC TRIBESMAN
The Gauls were iron-using people who came originally from an area north of the Alps. They settled throughout Europe after the 5th century BCE. The Romans regarded them as barbarians, given to fighting and boasting.

WALL OF DEFENCE
As the population of Rome grew, the city spread beyond its limits. The original wall, built in 378 BCE, remained Rome's only defence until Emperor Aurelian built new walls in 270 CE.

Over time, the Romans rebuilt the ruins of their city and regained the land they had lost. They were determined not to be defeated by setbacks and disasters. So, after the Gauls departed, the Romans intensified their military efforts and began to attack and take control of other territories in central Italy. They were now the greatest military power in the region. However, the invasion of the Gauls had been such a terrible blow to Roman pride that the Romans could not rest until they had conquered all of northern Italy.

About 20 years later, probably in 378 BCE, the Romans decided to build a new defensive wall around the city. It was constructed from great blocks of stone, taken from nearby quarries. The wall was 11 km (7 miles) long, and contained 21 gates to control access into the city. It was so well made that large sections of it survive to this day, almost 2,500 years after it was erected. However, the wall was expensive to build, and there are accounts that the plebeians grew angry when higher taxes were imposed on them to pay for it.

But in approximately 367 BCE, there was an act of union between the patricians and the plebeians. The patricians passed a series of measures allowing plebeians to put their names forward for the post of consul and for other senior positions. Certain wealthy plebeian families were also allowed to enter the Senate. The richer plebeians and the patricians became known as the *nobilita*s, or the nobility. For the time being, there appeared to be harmony between the patricians and the plebeians.

In later times, the Romans would come to regard the period of the early Republic as a golden age, when the traditional Roman virtues of honesty and frugality, modesty and bravery were seen at their best. The ideal Roman character was the farmer-soldier, who was always ready to put down his plough and take up his sword for the sake of Rome. The story was told of a Roman general named Cincinnatus, who was called from his plough and ordered to prepare and take command of an army to fight against the Aequi. He did so within 15 days and, after winning a famous victory, promptly went back to work on his farm. In the centuries to come, when life in Rome seemed too luxurious and too decadent, the Romans looked back on men like Cincinnatus with awe and respect.

HOSTILE HILLS
The Gauls who settled in northern Italy held out against the growing power of Rome. The Romans named the area inhabited by the Gauls as *Gallia Cisalpina*, meaning "Gaul this side of the Alps".

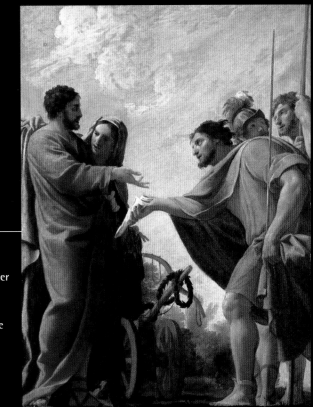

CINCINNATUS
This Italian painting shows Cincinnatus receiving the order to raise an army. In the early days of the Republic, only citizens who owned land were allowed to join the army.

CHAPTER TWO

The Warrior state

For two centuries, the Roman Republic was almost constantly at war. After taking control of Latium, the Romans went on to conquer the tribes of the surrounding regions – the Samnites to the east, the Volsci to the south and the Etruscans to the north.

PIECE BY PIECE, THE MIGHTY Roman army took over almost the entire peninsula of Italy. By the beginning of the 3rd century BCE, the only areas remaining outside Roman control were the parts of northern Italy inhabited by the Gauls, and the cities of the south, founded several centuries earlier by the Greeks.

The Romans were often generous to those they defeated. The inhabitants of many neighbouring towns were given full Roman citizenship. In return for serving in the army, citizens were protected by Roman law and could vote in the assemblies if they were resident in Rome. Other towns were given half-citizenship – their men had to serve in the Roman army, but they could not vote in the Roman assemblies. Most cities, however, were offered an alliance. This meant that they could govern themselves, keeping

◀ Mars, the god of war

VIA APPIA
This famous road was begun in 312 BCE under the censor Appius Claudius Caecus. It had a total length of 563 km (350 miles) and connected Rome to many strategic towns and ports.

control of their own coinage and their own taxation, but they had to provide soldiers for the Roman army. So, the Romans could count upon an immense number of soldiers to keep themselves in a position of power. The size of their army drove them on to conquer more land and to fight more wars, so gaining more plunder and more wealth. Rome had become a war machine.

As almost the whole of Italy came under Roman rule, there followed what has become known as the "Romanization" of the country. The Latin language of the Romans became the standard language for the entire country. The noblest families of Rome married into the most powerful and wealthy families of the conquered cities, thus creating ties of friendship and alliance. The Romans brought stability to most of Italy, and Rome assumed the role of protector, defending Italy against tribes of invading Gauls from the north. They built a vast network of roads that allowed their armies to move rapidly throughout Italy in case of attack or rebellion. The most

INTO BATTLE
Roman soldiers hurled their javelins at the enemy before charging forward with their swords at the ready.

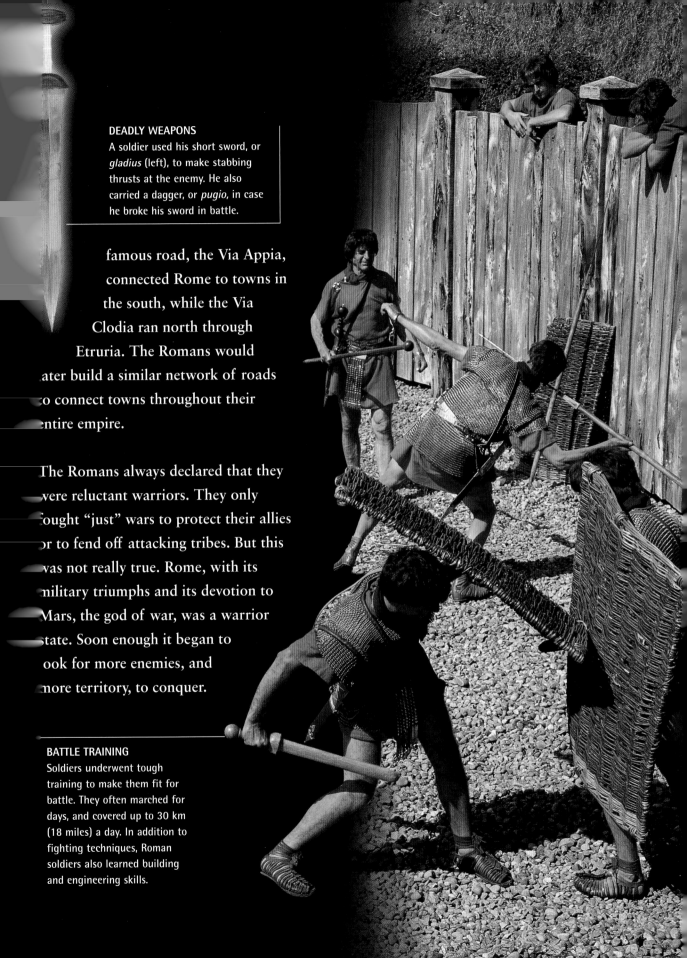

DEADLY WEAPONS
A soldier used his short sword, or *gladius* (left), to make stabbing thrusts at the enemy. He also carried a dagger, or *pugio*, in case he broke his sword in battle.

famous road, the Via Appia, connected Rome to towns in the south, while the Via Clodia ran north through Etruria. The Romans would later build a similar network of roads to connect towns throughout their entire empire.

The Romans always declared that they were reluctant warriors. They only fought "just" wars to protect their allies or to fend off attacking tribes. But this was not really true. Rome, with its military triumphs and its devotion to Mars, the god of war, was a warrior state. Soon enough it began to look for more enemies, and more territory, to conquer.

BATTLE TRAINING
Soldiers underwent tough training to make them fit for battle. They often marched for days, and covered up to 30 km (18 miles) a day. In addition to fighting techniques, Roman soldiers also learned building and engineering skills.

In 282 BCE, Rome turned its attentions to Magna Graecia (Greater Greece), the area that included the Greek cities of southern Italy as well as the island of Sicily. A king called Pyrrhus ruled the kingdom of Epirus in Greece. In 280 BCE, the Greek city of Tarentum, in the south of Italy, asked for Pyrrhus's help against the Romans. Pyrrhus brought a huge army that included 22,000 foot soldiers, 3,000 cavalry soldiers and 20 war elephants. The Roman soldiers were so terrified by the sight and smell of these great beasts that they fled in panic. Although Pyrrhus had defeated the Romans, he lost around 4,000 of his own soldiers during the battle, and is reported to have said, "Another victory like this, and I shall be ruined." The phrase "a Pyrrhic victory" is still sometimes used today to mean a victory that is won at too high a cost.

UNLUCKY PYRRHUS
After his defeat by the Romans, Pyrrhus left Italy for good. He then fought an unsuccessful war in Greece, before being killed in a street brawl.

The defeated Romans did not give up. They marched against Pyrrhus a second time and were beaten a second time. In the next battle, Pyrrhus's elephants were overwhelmed by the Roman soldiers and charged at their own side in terror. The Romans, at last the victors, later paraded eight of the captured elephants in triumph through the

streets of Rome. After that, most of the Greek cities in southern Italy made peace with Rome.

While Rome was extending its territory in Italy, the Carthaginians were gaining power in the western Mediterranean. The Carthaginians were a rich trading people, whose capital was Carthage on the coast of North Africa (present-day Tunisia). The Romans and the Carthaginians came into conflict over the island of Sicily. For a long time in Sicily, there had been an uneasy relationship between the cities that were governed by Greece and those that were allied to Carthage. The Romans feared that the Carthaginians wanted to control the whole of Sicily, and would then use the island to launch an invasion on Italy. In 264 BCE, Rome became involved in a conflict between Carthage and Messana, one of the Greek cities in Sicily. The fight over Messana led to a full-scale war with Carthage itself. This is known as the First Punic War, a name that derives from the word *Poeni*, the Latin name for the Carthaginians.

To fight the war, the Romans had to ferry their troops across the sea to Sicily. The Romans were not a seafaring people, and they had no fleet of ships. All their previous campaigns had been fought on land. But with characteristic determination, they decided that they needed to build a navy. By good fortune, they captured a Carthaginian ship

BEASTS OF WAR
This plate depicts a war elephant used during the Pyrrhic Wars. Elephants were specially trained to charge at the enemy.

GREEK INFLUENCE
Much of Roman architecture was influenced by the Greeks. These magnificent temples with massive columns are at Paestum, one of the Greek cities of southern Italy.

BATTLE AT SEA
The Romans used a drawbridge to storm a Carthaginian ship and overpower the enemy in fierce hand-to-hand fighting on deck.

that had run aground. They took it to bits, discovered how it worked and then copied it. The enemy ship was a *quinquereme* – a vessel with five banks of oars. Using it as a model, the Romans built 100 ships in 60 days. But the Romans added their own device called a *corvus* (which means "crow"). It was a grappling iron that kept an enemy ship close against the Roman ship.

The Romans fought their first ever naval battle off the coast of Sicily in 260 BCE. Knowing that the Romans had no experience of fighting at sea, the Carthaginians rowed their ships straight towards them to ram and sink their vessels. But the Romans used their new "crows" to grab and hold the Carthaginian ships. The Romans then boarded the enemy ships and fought on the decks, using their traditional battle skills. As a result, 50 ships were taken and 10,000 Carthaginians were captured or killed. The Romans had convincingly won their first battle at sea.

VICTORY COIN
The Romans boasted of their great victory over Carthage by issuing a gold coin stamped with the image of a warship.

Carthage was a trading empire. It relied upon the sea, and it needed ships to take supplies to its

The Romans at sea

The Roman warship was little more than a floating platform on which the soldiers could be brought into close contact with the enemy. For this purpose, the Romans invented a huge boarding plank with a large spike on the end, which could be raised and lowered like a drawbridge. The spike would embed itself into the enemy's deck and the legionaries could board the enemy vessel across it. When the Romans were not fighting sea battles, their fleet patrolled the Mediterranean for pirates.

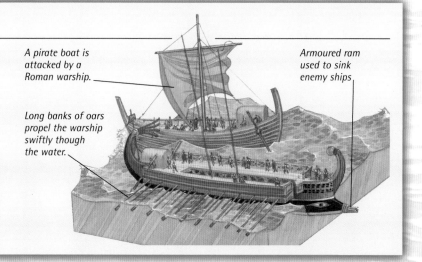

A pirate boat is attacked by a Roman warship.

Long banks of oars propel the warship swiftly though the water.

Armoured ram used to sink enemy ships

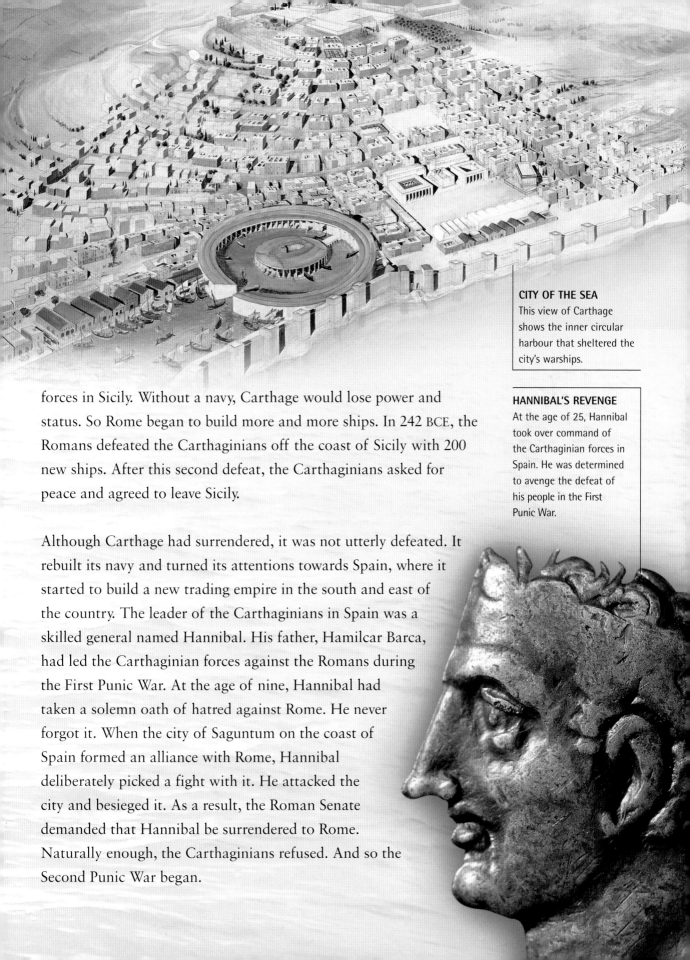

CITY OF THE SEA
This view of Carthage shows the inner circular harbour that sheltered the city's warships.

HANNIBAL'S REVENGE
At the age of 25, Hannibal took over command of the Carthaginian forces in Spain. He was determined to avenge the defeat of his people in the First Punic War.

forces in Sicily. Without a navy, Carthage would lose power and status. So Rome began to build more and more ships. In 242 BCE, the Romans defeated the Carthaginians off the coast of Sicily with 200 new ships. After this second defeat, the Carthaginians asked for peace and agreed to leave Sicily.

Although Carthage had surrendered, it was not utterly defeated. It rebuilt its navy and turned its attentions towards Spain, where it started to build a new trading empire in the south and east of the country. The leader of the Carthaginians in Spain was a skilled general named Hannibal. His father, Hamilcar Barca, had led the Carthaginian forces against the Romans during the First Punic War. At the age of nine, Hannibal had taken a solemn oath of hatred against Rome. He never forgot it. When the city of Saguntum on the coast of Spain formed an alliance with Rome, Hannibal deliberately picked a fight with it. He attacked the city and besieged it. As a result, the Roman Senate demanded that Hannibal be surrendered to Rome. Naturally enough, the Carthaginians refused. And so the Second Punic War began.

Hannibal devised an ambitious plan. He would not wait for the Romans to attack his bases in Spain. He would take the battle to them and invade Italy. So, Hannibal marched with 50,000 men and 37 war elephants along the coast of Spain, through the Pyrenees and along the southern coast of France. His plan was to cross the Alps and swoop down on Rome from the north.

ELEPHANT ARMY
Many of the huge beasts died of cold and terror as they slipped and slid their way over the frozen mountain passes.

ALPINE MOUNTAINS
By the time Hannibal reached the Alps, it was October, and the mountains were already deep in snow, making the journey even more treacherous.

Hannibal's journey through the Alps has become the subject of many legends and stories. His army had to cross over dangerous passes and withstand the attacks of hardy mountain tribes, who rolled down great boulders upon them. Some 24,000 men – almost half the entire army – died in the mountains. Yet Hannibal's army came through, and within two months, had taken almost the whole of northern Italy. After losing a great battle at Lake Trasimene, the Romans withdrew their forces from the north. The Gauls of the region, traditional enemies of Rome, flocked to join Hannibal's side. It was a perilous moment. Fabius, the Roman general in command, waited in an attempt to buy time and wear down Hannibal's army. His tactics earned him the name "*Cunctator*", or "Delayer".

Then the Romans made a mistake. They abandoned Fabius's waiting game and decided to overwhelm Hannibal by force of

arms. They sent 50,000 men to fight against him at a place called Cannae, but Hannibal defeated them, and almost all the Roman soldiers were killed. It was a great disaster, and some of the cities of southern Italy now decided to make their peace with Hannibal. The Roman Senate, however, remained firm. They refused to negotiate with Hannibal and refused to ransom the few Roman prisoners who were left alive.

Having failed to defeat Hannibal in Italy, the Romans sent an army into Spain under the command of a 25-year-old general named Scipio. After defeating the Carthaginians in Spain, Scipio went on to invade North Africa. In 202 BCE, Hannibal hurried back from Italy to face him, but he was utterly defeated by Scipio's army at Zama in Tunisia. Although Hannibal escaped, he later committed suicide to avoid being captured by the Romans. Once more, the Carthaginians were forced to make peace on humiliating terms. They had to reduce their once-proud navy to a fleet of just ten ships, give up all claims to Spain and pay a huge fine to the Romans. Worse was to follow.

SAVIOUR OF ROME
Scipio was given the surname "Africanus" in honour of his victorious campaign in North Africa, where he triumphed over Hannibal.

Although the Carthaginians were no longer a threat to Rome, the Romans had not forgotten Hannibal and their defeats at his hands. Throughout this period, a Roman statesman named Cato ended every speech he made with the phrase "Carthage must be destroyed." When the Carthaginians acquired another army, in defiance of the treaty with Rome, the Romans took this opportunity to declare war. They would only hold back, the Senate said, if the Carthaginians left Carthage altogether. Of course this demand was utterly unacceptable – it would mean the end of Carthaginian civilization itself. And so the people of Carthage began hastily to fortify their city.

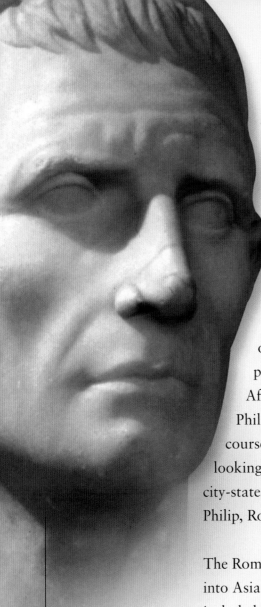

In 149 BCE, the Romans sent an army to Carthage. After a siege that lasted almost three years, the city eventually fell to the Romans. Carthage was utterly destroyed and all its inhabitants were massacred or sold into slavery.

The mighty Romans now controlled the entire western Mediterranean. But they still looked for new lands to conquer and had already turned their eyes towards the northern kingdom of Macedon in Greece. Philip V, the king of Macedon, ruled all of Greece and considered himself the protector of the Greek cities of Sicily and southern Italy. After Hannibal's stunning victory over the Romans at Cannae, Philip had made an alliance with the Carthaginians. This, of course, had aroused the anger of the Romans, and they were looking for an opportunity for revenge. When several of the Greek city-states appealed to Rome for help against a possible invasion from Philip, Rome sent in its forces and defeated Philip in 197 BCE.

ANTIOCHUS THE GREAT
An ambitious king of Syria, Antiochus dreamed of reviving the empire of Alexander the Great. He ended up losing his own kingdom to the mighty power of Rome.

The Romans then withdrew their forces from Greece and marched into Asia to fight King Antiochus III, who ruled a large kingdom that included Persia, southern Syria, Palestine and part of Asia Minor. After Philip's defeat, Antiochus had tried to extend his empire by invading Greece, but had been defeated by the Romans. In 190 BCE, the Romans followed Antiochus to Asia and destroyed his army during a great battle at Magnesia in Asia Minor. The Romans now had control of large stretches of Asia, and it appeared that no force on earth could stop them now.

Although the Romans handed over much of their conquered territory to the authority of local rulers, they never fully withdrew from any country they had defeated. They continued to meddle in Greek affairs and, in 168 BCE, they took direct control of Macedon. In

146 BCE, Rome squashed a rebellion in the Greek city of Corinth, and in a display of naked power and brutality, Roman soldiers destroyed the city and sold its inhabitants into slavery, just as they had done in Carthage. By 145 BCE, Rome controlled the whole of Greece.

After these victories the Romans grew ever more confident and aggressive. In the lands they conquered, they became known for their cruelty and for their arrogance. Some Roman governors, known as *praetors*, used their office to exploit the resources of conquered territories and make themselves enormously rich. Many Roman historians agreed that, after the fall of Carthage, Rome had become too preoccupied with money and with luxury. Driven by ambition and the greed for power, individuals worked for their own benefit rather than for the good of the Republic. This would lead to serious civil strife in the years to come.

FALLEN CITY
After the Romans had destroyed the city of Carthage, they spread salt over the ground so that nothing would ever grow there again.

A VAST EMPIRE
As a result of many years of warfare, Rome had acquired vast amounts of territory. Rome's growth began with the gradual conquest of Italy. By 100 BCE, it ruled over much of the Mediterranean coast and governed land stretching from Spain as far as Asia.

■ **Extent of the Roman empire in 100 BCE**

Gaul

Alps

Spain

Italy

Corsica

Saguntum ■

■ Rome

■ Cannae

Macedonia

Sardinia

■ Corinth

■ Pergamum

Greece

■ Cilicia

Carthage ■

Sicily

North Africa

Mediterranean Sea

CHAPTER THREE

Republican Rome

After years of war, the city of Rome was now the centre of an empire in all but name. By the end of the 2nd century BCE, it controlled all of Italy and Greece, most of Spain, parts of North Africa and Asia Minor, and the southern part of Gaul.

THE CAPITAL OF AN EMPIRE becomes the home for hundreds of different peoples and ethnic groups. Rome was a haven for merchants and envoys, poets and orators, and musicians and dancing girls from all over the known world. Some came looking for financial support from Rome's rich citizens, others came in search of employment and profit.

The city had grown rapidly in size and in population, and was now one of the largest cities of the Mediterranean world. It was also one of the wealthiest, as riches poured in from lands conquered by the Romans. The Senate began to grow concerned that too much luxury would weaken the life of the Republic. Laws were passed against the obvious display of wealth, such as the wearing of variously coloured robes and gold jewellery. But these measures had very little effect

SEGOVIAN AQUEDUCT
This stone aqueduct in Segovia, Spain, was built in the 2nd century CE and has 128 arches. The water was carried 30 m (98 ft) above the ground along the top tier of the aqueduct.

THE ROMAN FORUM
This view shows the Via Sacra, the ancient street running through the Roman Forum. The three tall columns are part of a temple dedicated to the gods Castor and Pollux.

Rome's public buildings symbolized the city's growing wealth and power. New stone streets and bridges were built to help ease congestion. In the Forum, the Romans built large rectangular buildings called basilicas – spacious indoor halls that were used as law courts and for public functions. But perhaps the most remarkable feats of engineering were the viaducts and aqueducts. The viaducts carried roads high above the ground, while the aqueducts supplied the city with fresh water. In the beginning, water was diverted from streams in the mountains outside Rome and brought to the city along stone channels beneath the ground. Later, the channels were raised on stone arches that tilted slightly downwards to maintain a constant flow of water. A reservoir called a *castellum aquae* collected the water, which was then sent through pipes to public fountains, private houses and the public baths.

Many new temples were also constructed, largely from public funds swollen by the profits of war. But it was not all good news in Rome. The city was overcrowded, dirty and unhealthy. The Senate was so preoccupied with the affairs of the state that it did little to improve the lives of

ordinary people. As the population soared, more space was needed for housing, and land grew very expensive. Only the privileged few could afford to live in town houses. The poor were crowded into tiny rooms in tenement buildings, called *insulae*. These buildings were often shoddily constructed and perilously unsafe.

At any one time, there were almost 100,000 male Romans on active service in the army, most of whom were farmers. While the farmers were away, slaves were used to farm the land in their place. The Roman economy depended on a steady supply of foreign slaves. They were organized into gangs and employed on a variety of tasks from quarrying stone to pruning vines. In Rome itself, wealthy citizens owned large numbers of slaves to work in the house and garden.

HOMES OF THE POOR
Many *insulae* were made of flimsy wood and were several storeys high. Few rooms had any heating, and water had to be carried up from the public fountains.

NARROW STREETS
City streets were just wide enough for carts to pass through, with houses jutting out over the pavements.

ARISTOCRATIC RULERS
Senators were elected for life and were chosen from wealthy Roman families. These senators are probably from the time of the emperor Hadrian, who brought beards into fashion. Senators in the early Republic were nearly always clean-shaven.

Although the political system had remained more or less unchanged since the early years of the Republic, it had become corrupt. In theory, the Senate managed the government of the city, while the plebeian assemblies approved or rejected new laws. However, some of Rome's richest families were able to control the government for long periods of time using their wealth to influence the elections of senators and magistrates. So, despite the people's assemblies, Rome was in fact ruled by a small, yet powerful, group (this type of government, where the few rule over the many, is called an oligarchy).

The Forum

At the heart of the city of Rome was the Forum. Similar to a town square, it was a place to meet friends, to discuss political events and to observe religious ceremonies to the gods. Clustered around it were public buildings, such as temples, assembly halls, courthouses and bathhouses. At one end was the *curia*, or Senate House. Politicians gave speeches from platforms in the Forum, and Romans gathered here to watch religious processions, victory parades and executions. The Forum was even home to gladiator contests and wild beast shows.

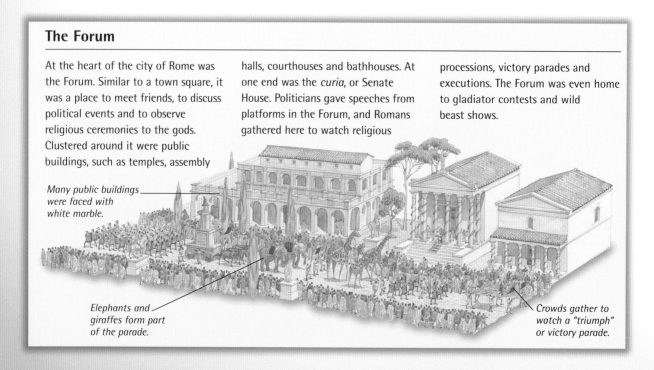

Many public buildings were faced with white marble.

Elephants and giraffes form part of the parade.

Crowds gather to watch a "triumph" or victory parade.

During this period, Rome was almost constantly at war. When a general returned to Rome from a victorious campaign abroad, the Senate would grant him a victory parade called a triumph. Standing in a chariot pulled by four horses, he led his soldiers through the principal streets of Rome, while acknowledging the cheers of the crowd. Also in the procession were captive enemy leaders and prisoners of war who were forced to endure the jeers and insults of the people. During the procession, the general and his army marched

CIRCUS MAXIMUS
One of the most popular spectator sports was chariot racing, which took place at racetracks called circuses. The Circus Maximus was the largest racetrack in Rome, holding up to 250,000 people.

to the Temple of Jupiter on the Capitol to pay homage to the king of the gods. The general wore red clothes and had his face painted red, in imitation of the statue of Jupiter that stood within the temple. It is said that a slave was placed beside him to whisper, "Look around and remember that you are a man," while soldiers shouted abuse to remind him that he was mortal. Victory celebrations could last for days and were one of the great events of the city's life.

HONOURING THE GODS
A Roman father, his head covered, throws salt into the fire. This solemn ritual was performed every day to honour Vesta, goddess of the hearth and household. It was very important that these rituals were conducted with the utmost precision, with the exact form of words being repeated at the right time.

Lavish public games and shows punctuated daily life in Rome. They might be held to celebrate a glorious victory or to mark the funeral of a particularly important citizen. The earliest games were running contests and chariot races, which took place in the Circus Maximus. Later, the Romans developed a taste for gladiator fights and wild beast hunts. The contests and public shows were paid for by the Senate or by private individuals who wished to win favour with their fellow citizens by performing great acts of generosity.

Religious festivals were at the heart of Roman society. All Romans were expected to worship the state gods who protected the city, and special ceremonies were performed to ensure their continuing goodwill. Religious rituals were carried out by specially trained

CULT OF VESTA
The Temple of Vesta in the Roman Forum was served by six women called the Vestal Virgins. They were the only women in the Roman religious system.

priests appointed by the state. The Senate elected individuals from among Rome's leading citizens to hold the office of *pontifex*, or priest. There were 16 priests altogether, and the priest who had the highest responsibility in religious matters was known as the *pontifex maximus*. The priests asked for the blessings of the gods by offering them animal sacrifices. The sacrificial victim – an ox, pig, sheep or chicken – was chosen with much care. Wine and sacred cornmeal were placed on the animal's head before it was killed with a single blow on an open-air altar. Its internal organs were then burned on the altar, so that the rising smoke could carry the sacrificial offering to the world of the gods.

No public activity or public decision was taken without the advice of special priests known as *augures* (augurs). Their role was to try to discover the will of the gods. They did this by examining unusual patterns made by birds, clouds or stars. They also observed displays of thunder and lightning, which were thought to hold messages from the gods. In addition, there were priests known as *haruscipes*, who examined the intestines of sacrificed animals for special messages or signs.

Generally, women did not feature in the public rituals of Rome. However, one group of priestesses, known as the Vestal Virgins, devoted their lives to Vesta, the goddess of the hearth and home. The priestesses lived in a special enclosure beside the Temple of Vesta in the Forum and were responsible for keeping the shrine's sacred fire alight. The Romans believed that if the flame went out, disaster would fall upon the city. The Vestal Virgins were

HIGH PRIEST
This statue shows the emperor Augustus dressed as the *pontifex maximus*. His head is covered, and he holds a libation bowl for pouring wine or oil as an offering to the gods.

selected from aristocratic families and were dressed as brides, although they were not allowed to marry. Any priestess who broke the sacred laws of Vesta was punished by being buried alive.

The Romans worshipped hundreds of different gods and goddesses, each with their own temples and rituals. The king of the gods was Jupiter, the sky-god. There were also the two great goddesses of the Roman world – Juno, the queen of heaven, and Minerva, the goddess of wisdom. Each god was responsible for a different aspect of life. There was Mars, the god of war, Bacchus, the god of wine, and Ceres, the goddess of agriculture. But the Romans did not only worship the gods of their ancestors. As they conquered new lands, they began to adopt the gods of the peoples they conquered. Sometimes, they identified a foreign god with one of their own deities. So, for example, the great Carthaginian god, Moloch, merged with the Roman god Saturn. But most Roman gods were borrowed from the Greeks. Amongst others, they adopted Asclepius, the god of healing, and Apollo, the god of the sun and patron of the arts.

In times of need, the Romans could turn to a particular god for help and assistance. If their

KING OF THE GODS
Jupiter was the god of the sky and the weather, and his symbols were the eagle and the thunderbolt. He later became identified with the Greek god Zeus.

SPECIAL TALISMAN
Many Romans carried lucky charms to ward off evil spirits. The symbols on this strange bronze hand – including a snake and a pine cone balanced on the thumb – were thought to have special powers.

prayers were answered, they would make a private offering to the god and put up an inscription of thanks. Offerings ranged from coins and brooches left by the poor to silver statues donated by the rich.

For major decisions, many Romans travelled to Greece to consult the oracle of Apollo at Delphi. The Romans thought that the gods could give them practical help in the form of oracles – forecasts and advice from priests or priestesses who acted as mouthpieces for the gods. The questions they asked were strictly practical, such as "Will I get divorced?" or "Will I become a magistrate?" Many Romans also visited soothsayers who claimed to be able to see into the future, or consulted astrologers who studied the movement of the planets and devised horoscopes for their clients.

But not all Romans believed in the gods. Indeed, some educated and cultured Romans publicly doubted their existence, and looked instead to the ideas of Greek philosophers, such as Socrates and Plato, to bring them happiness and peace of mind. They would have special need of this in the coming century as the Republic was about to enter a long period of crisis and alarm.

Household gods

Every house had a shrine called a *lararium*. Here, the family worshipped the household spirits that protected the home from evil. The gods who looked after the house were called *lares* and *penates*. *Lares* guarded the boundaries of the home and all who lived within them, while the *penates* took care of the cupboards of stored food. Roman families also had a duty to remember their ancestors, and wax masks or portraits were given places of honour in the home.

Statue of a genius, an individual's guardian spirit

Snakes were thought to protect dwelling places.

Household shrines were often shaped like temples.

CHAPTER FOUR

Turmoil *engulfs* *the* Republic

At the end of the 2nd century BCE, the Roman Republic faced a series of crises from which it never recovered. The turmoil began with two ambitious brothers named Gracchus, who tried to change the system of government for their own ends.

THE ELDER OF THE TWO brothers, Tiberius Gracchus, was elected a tribune in 133 BCE. He championed the poor against the rich, partly out of concern for their plight, but more probably to advance his own career. He proposed a law that took land from the rich and gave it to the poor. Naturally, Tiberius made many enemies, especially among the rich landowners who stood to lose large parts of their estates. When, in defiance of all custom, Tiberius stood for election as tribune for a second year, Rome erupted into violence. A group of senators opposed to his reforms started a riot, during which Tiberius was killed.

In 123 BCE, Tiberius's brother, Gaius Gracchus, was elected a tribune. He proposed measures to give cheaper grain to the poor and more power to the people's assemblies. Once

◀ Vercingetorix surrenders to Julius Caesar

BROTHERLY LOVE
This statue shows the
Gracchus brothers at the
knee of their mother,
Cornelia. It is said that
Gaius ordered a slave
to stab him to death to
avoid being captured.

more, attempts at reform led to violence. In 121 BCE, Gaius was killed, and several thousand of his supporters were captured and executed. The fate of both brothers showed that deep hostility had grown between the poor and the nobility (the patricians and wealthy plebeians). Men like the Gracchus brothers were ready to further their own ambitions by claiming to be friends of the people. The nobility were ready to use violence to defend their privileges.

As Rome continued to extend its empire, a successful general named Gaius Marius decided to reform the Roman army. In the early days of the Republic, only citizens who owned land were allowed to enlist. In times of conflict, citizen-farmers left their land and assembled to fight using their own weapons. But once Rome became involved in long overseas wars, the farmers had to leave their land for years on end. They often fell into debt, and their farms were sold off to rich landowners. In the 2nd century BCE, Marius reorganized the army, allowing all citizens to enlist, whether they owned land or not. He provided weapons for all soldiers and introduced a tough system of arms training (adopted from gladiator schools). With this new army, Marius won notable victories in North Africa and in northern Italy. For a while, his success made him the most important man in Rome.

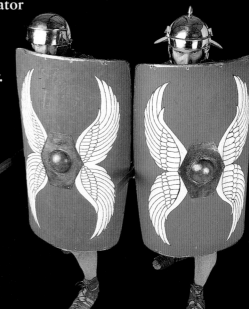

AMBITIOUS LEADER
Marius was appointed consul seven times. He was hailed as the third founder of Rome, and his career had a profound effect on his nephew Julius Caesar.

ARMY REFORMER
One of Marius's reforms was the introduction the century, a fighting unit of 80 men. His soldiers were called "Marius's mules" because of the heavy equipment they had to carry.

PLUMED HELMET
Roman officers wore a
crest on their helmets, so
that their men could see
them in the thick of battle.

Before long, Rome faced another severe test.
In 91 BCE, a tribune, Marcus Livius Drusus,
proposed a law giving citizenship to all
Italian cities allied to Rome. The Senate
rejected the proposal, and Drusus was killed
by an unknown assassin. Disappointed that
they had lost the chance to become Roman
citizens, the Italian allies revolted against
their Roman masters and began what
was known as the Social War (from the
Latin word *socius* meaning "ally"). The allied forces were
well trained, and the Roman army suffered heavy losses
during the course of the campaign. The war finally
ended when the Romans gave full citizenship to all
the Italian cities.

But worse was to come, for Rome now faced
the first civil war in its history. In
88 BCE, a young consul named Sulla
had been given charge of an army
to fight Mithridates, the king of
Pontus (now part of Turkey). But
at the last moment, the
command was switched to

SAMNITE WARRIOR
The Samnites were one of the tribes who fought in
the Social War against Marius. Later, Marius included
Samnite warriors in the forces he led against his
bitter rival Sulla.

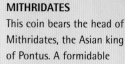

MITHRIDATES
This coin bears the head of Mithridates, the Asian king of Pontus. A formidable enemy of the Romans, he was eventually defeated by Pompey in Asia Minor.

General Marius. In a fury, Sulla turned and led his troops into Rome itself. Marius was forced to flee, and his supporters were executed.

DICTATOR OF ROME
Sulla was the first dictator of Rome to have no fixed period of office (usually dictators were appointed in times of crisis for a maximum period of six months). He was also the first Roman to invade his own city. During his reign of terror, he had hundreds of citizens beheaded and their heads nailed up in the city centre.

After Marius had fled, Sulla left Rome and marched his army to Pontus to fight Mithridates. While Sulla was away, Marius returned from exile and took control of the city, murdering hundreds of Sulla's allies. Marius died in 86 BCE, but when Sulla returned to Italy, he found that his properties had been confiscated and that Marius's supporters were in power. Sulla fled Rome, but returned three years later to exact a terrible revenge. A true reign of terror began in the city. Death squads rounded up Sulla's enemies and murdered them without trial. Many people were executed because of their wealth or their property. Throughout this bloodbath, Sulla claimed that he was merely defending the Republic against its enemies. In 82 BCE, he made himself dictator, or sole ruler, of Rome. During Sulla's dictatorship, peace did eventually return to Rome. But no one would ever forget the bloody days of his rule.

Sulla's career signalled that the path to power lay with the generals who commanded the most powerful armies. The generals were more like warlords, whose grasp on power depended on fighting and winning battles. After Sulla's departure, two of his supporters, Pompey and Crassus, combined their joint forces to rule Rome. There were enemies to fight in all parts of the empire, including pirates who were attacking Roman ships in the Mediterranean. But first, there was one threat to deal with much nearer home.

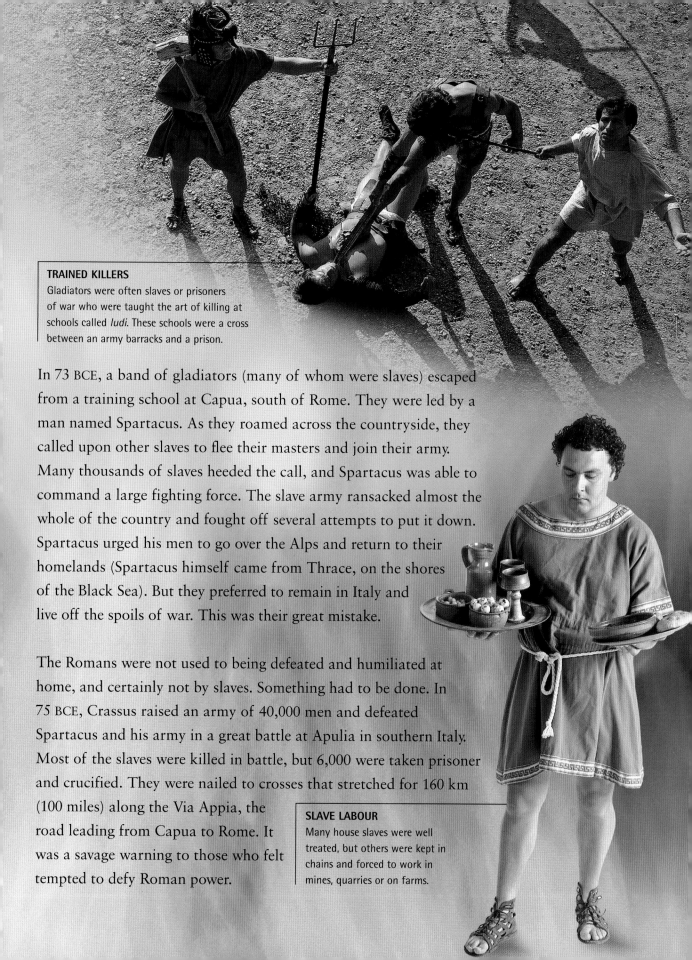

TRAINED KILLERS
Gladiators were often slaves or prisoners of war who were taught the art of killing at schools called *ludi*. These schools were a cross between an army barracks and a prison.

In 73 BCE, a band of gladiators (many of whom were slaves) escaped from a training school at Capua, south of Rome. They were led by a man named Spartacus. As they roamed across the countryside, they called upon other slaves to flee their masters and join their army. Many thousands of slaves heeded the call, and Spartacus was able to command a large fighting force. The slave army ransacked almost the whole of the country and fought off several attempts to put it down. Spartacus urged his men to go over the Alps and return to their homelands (Spartacus himself came from Thrace, on the shores of the Black Sea). But they preferred to remain in Italy and live off the spoils of war. This was their great mistake.

The Romans were not used to being defeated and humiliated at home, and certainly not by slaves. Something had to be done. In 75 BCE, Crassus raised an army of 40,000 men and defeated Spartacus and his army in a great battle at Apulia in southern Italy. Most of the slaves were killed in battle, but 6,000 were taken prisoner and crucified. They were nailed to crosses that stretched for 160 km (100 miles) along the Via Appia, the road leading from Capua to Rome. It was a savage warning to those who felt tempted to defy Roman power.

SLAVE LABOUR
Many house slaves were well treated, but others were kept in chains and forced to work in mines, quarries or on farms.

JULIUS CAESAR
Caesar was well connected in Rome. He was the nephew of General Marius, and his daughter Julia was the wife of Pompey.

A third man now emerged to challenge Crassus and Pompey for the leadership of Rome. His name was Julius Caesar, and he would prove more ambitious and more successful than either. Caesar came from a patrician family and began his career as an orator, or speech-maker. He rose to power rapidly, first becoming *pontifex maximus*, then *praetor*. In 60 BCE, he formed an alliance with Pompey and Crassus, and was elected consul the following year. To win over the people of Rome, Caesar spent lavishly on public buildings and free gladiator shows. When he could not get his way by persuasion, he was quite prepared to use troops to bully the members of the Senate. During his consulship, he was made governor of Gaul for a period of five years. It was the beginning of a career that has become part of history itself.

The country the Romans knew as Gaul was roughly the area of France and Belgium today. It was inhabited by a tribe of Celtic people known as the Gauls. When Caesar became governor in 58 BCE, the Romans ruled only a small part of southern Gaul around the mouth of the River Rhône. They were under constant threat of attack by tribes from the northern regions. Caesar led a campaign to push back the invading tribes, and after a series of great victories, he conquered central and northern Gaul, extending Roman territory as far as the English Channel. In six years, he had brought a huge country and its population under Roman control. He later wrote an account of his exploits in which he gives a vivid picture of Roman soldiers in action.

Caesar's victories in Gaul had made him extremely rich, and his success in battle had earned him the unswerving devotion and loyalty of his men. By now, Crassus had been killed in battle in the East, and Pompey, once Caesar's patron, had become his great rival. Pompey's forces far outnumbered Caesar's, but they were scattered all over the Republic. It was time for Caesar to return to Rome, where he could expect to fulfil his destiny as a great leader.

VERCINGETORIX
After Caesar crushed the Gauls at the Battle of Alesia, their defeated leader, Vercingetorix, laid down his weapons at Caesar's feet. He was taken to Rome in chains and executed.

BATTLE SCENE
When Roman troops stormed a fortified town, they dragged a wheeled siege tower against the wall. Some soldiers stormed over the walls on a drawbridge lowered from the siege tower, while others smashed holes in the walls with battering rams.

QUEEN CLEOPATRA
Famed for her intelligence
and charm, Cleopatra was of
Greek descent, but she spoke
Egyptian and considered
herself daughter of Ra, the
Egyptian sun-god.

NO TURNING BACK
Once Caesar's army
had crossed the bridge
over the Rubicon into Italy,
civil war was inevitable.

Such a rich and powerful man was bound to stir up enemies, however, and the senators in Rome began to fear Caesar's growing power. The Senate proposed that he should be stripped of his command and that his army should be disbanded. Realizing that he was not going to defeat his enemies from a distance, he chose the perilous course of invading Rome itself, just as Sulla had done before him. So, Julius Caesar marched with his army from Gaul into northern Italy until he reached a small stream known as the Rubicon, which formed the border between Gaul and Italy. There he paused. "We can still draw back," he told his colleagues. "But once we have crossed this little bridge, we shall have to fight." He crossed, and ever since that time, the phrase "to cross the Rubicon" means to take a decision from which there is no going back. The news of Caesar's arrival in Italy caused his enemies to flee Rome. He invaded the city and took control of it without bloodshed. Then, he followed Pompey to Greece, where he defeated him in battle. Pompey fled to Alexandria in Egypt, but was murdered shortly before Caesar arrived in pursuit.

During his time in Egypt, Caesar fell under the spell of its young queen, Cleopatra. She had been ousted from the throne of Egypt shortly before, and was battling with her brother Ptolemy for the throne. With Caesar's support, she was able to regain her power. Cleopatra has become one of the great legends of the classical world – a queen whose intelligence was equal to her beauty. It is said that she was presented to Caesar while rolled up in a purple carpet (purple being the colour of royalty). Certainly her charms were such that she became Caesar's mistress and bore his son.

EGYPTIAN QUEEN
This relief of Cleopatra is from the temple of Hathor in Egypt. Cleopatra (left) is dressed as the Egyptian goddess, Isis.

After an absence of more than three years, Caesar eventually returned to Rome, having defeated all of his enemies. As part of the lavish victory celebrations, he staged spectacular parades, games and public feasts. He rewarded every member of his infantry with 240 gold pieces. He also gave every Roman citizen four gold pieces, in addition to large quantities of grain and oil. In one procession, his triumphal wagons carried a sign bearing the words, "Veni, Vidi, Vici" – "I came, I saw, I conquered." These have become the most famous Latin words in history.

Now that Caesar was in a position of absolute power, he began to pass new laws and impose changes. He planned canals and libraries, reformed the calendar and the legal system, and took steps to improve the sanitation of Rome. But in spite of these good works, there were many people in Rome who considered him a tyrant.

There were good reasons for thinking that he had become too proud. He was given the title "Father of the Country" and a golden throne was erected for him in the Senate. People even began to compare him to a god. The seventh month of the year was renamed "Julius" in his honour – the month that we still call "July" today.

Cicero, statesman and orator

Marcus Tullius Cicero (104–43 BCE) was an outstanding politician and orator. Julius Caesar found Cicero a powerful opponent in Senate meetings and tried several times to form an alliance with him. Cicero mistrusted Caesar's desire for supreme power and refused. He eventually withdrew from politics to live in the country, where he wrote books on oratory and philosophy. After Caesar's death, Cicero delivered speeches against Mark Antony, and was eventually murdered by Mark Antony's troops.

READY MONEY
Caesar was the first living Roman to issue a coin bearing his portrait – an honour that was usually only awarded to famous Romans after their death.

HIDDEN DANGER

Caesar's enemies plotted to kill him as he entered the Senate. Each of them agreed to stab him so they would all share the blame. They hid their daggers beforehand in the boxes that held official papers for the meeting.

Under Caesar's rule, the Republic ceased to exist in all but name. He alone controlled the government and the armies of Rome. In 44 BCE, he became dictator (sole ruler) for life. It was even said that he wanted to take the title of *rex* or king. Ever since the end of the monarchy 500 years before, Romans had scorned the idea of being ruled by a king, and this was too much for many to bear. So, a band of 60 senators conspired to assassinate Caesar. Some of them had been his friends and colleagues, but they were all united in hatred of his tyranny. On the day known as

THE CRUELLEST BLOW

A group of assassins, led by the senator Cassius, struck a series of fatal blows. When Caesar saw his friend Brutus among the attackers, he called out "*Et tu, Brute!*", which means "You too, Brutus!"

the Ides of March (15th March), the conspirators surrounded Caesar as he entered the Senate and stabbed him 33 times with daggers they had hidden under their togas. At the age of 55, the father of his country was dead. He had been stirred by ambition and the desire for power, and captivated by the idea of glory and immortal fame. He had a vision of Rome restored, risen from the wreckage of the Republic, but he did not live to fulfil it. His name, however, has survived. To this day he remains the best known of all Roman leaders.

BATTLE OF ACTIUM
Mark Antony was defeated by
Octavian at the Battle of Actium. After
his defeat, Mark Antony fled to Egypt
with Cleopatra. When Octavian
pursued them there, they both
committed suicide.

There immediately followed another bitter struggle for power.
Caesar's fellow consul was Marcus Antonius (usually known as Mark
Antony), but his chosen heir was Octavian, his 19-year-old nephew
and adopted son. Octavian joined forces with Mark Antony and his
ally Aemilius Lepidus to hunt down the conspirators. They avenged
Caesar's murder with more bloodshed, killing 2,000 people.

It was perhaps inevitable that as soon as Octavian, Mark Antony and
Lepidus had achieved their goal, they would start fighting one
another. Lepidus was given charge of North Africa, while Octavian
and Mark Antony divided the rest of the empire between them. Mark
Antony ruled the East, and Octavian ruled the West, sharing power
uneasily for almost 12 years. Their alliance ended in 31 BCE when
Octavian defeated Mark Antony in a sea-battle at Actium, off the
coast of Greece, and made himself the undisputed ruler of the
Roman empire.

THE FIRST EMPEROR
Octavian, Caesar's nephew
and successor, ruled Rome
for 44 years and was given
the name of Augustus.
When Augustus became
the first emperor, he knew
that people would be
concerned that Rome was
returning to the rule of
kings, so he called himself
princeps or "first citizen".

Octavian maintained his position of
supreme power for the next 44 years.
Order was finally restored to the
Roman world after decades of civil
strife. Octavian became known as
Caesar Augustus – the first name in
honour of Julius Caesar, and the
second name meaning "revered". He
also used the title *imperator* (victor in
battle), from which we get our word
emperor. It was a decisive turning point
in the history of Rome. From this time
forward began the reign of the emperors.

CHAPTER FIVE

The *early* emperors

Augustus was a wise and efficient ruler, who brought peace to Rome after decades of civil war. The Roman Republic was over, and the period of history known as the empire had begun. Rome was to be ruled by emperors for the next 500 years.

AUGUSTUS DECLARED THAT HE had handed the Republic back to the care of the Senate and people of Rome. He made an outward show of consulting the Senate, but in fact, Augustus kept total control of the empire. He was the supreme general of the Roman army and senior governor of the imperial provinces. He was also

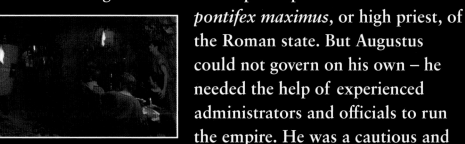

pontifex maximus, or high priest, of the Roman state. But Augustus could not govern on his own – he needed the help of experienced administrators and officials to run the empire. He was a cautious and practical man, whose aim was to put the Roman state on a solid foundation for the future. Although he held absolute power, he was good-natured and well disposed to those around him. He could on occasions be ruthless, but he would have claimed that his ruthlessness was for the general good of the state.

◀ The first emperor, Augustus

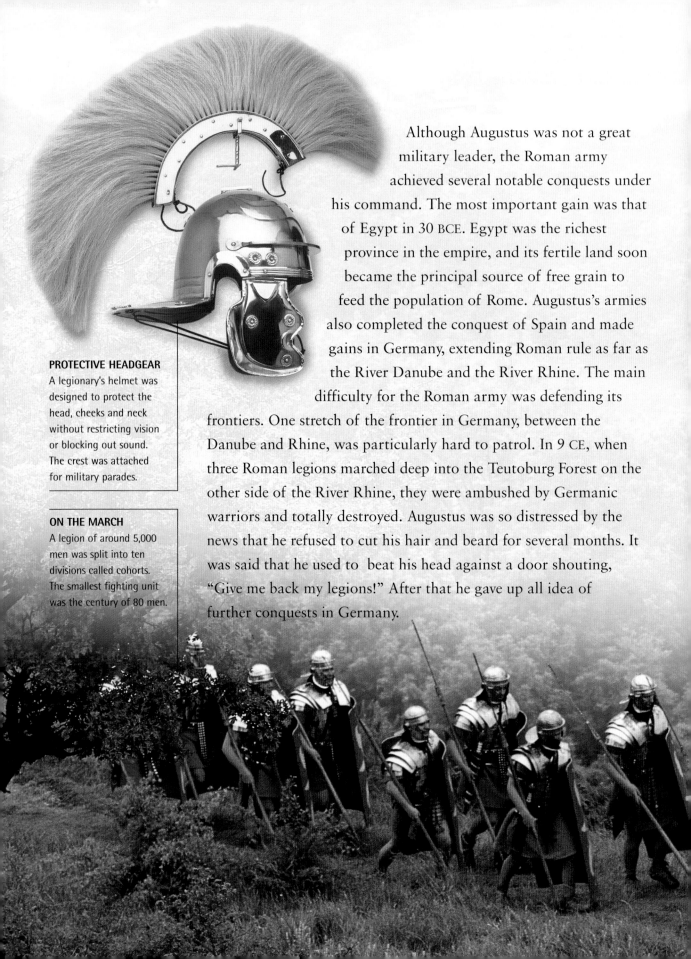

Although Augustus was not a great military leader, the Roman army achieved several notable conquests under his command. The most important gain was that of Egypt in 30 BCE. Egypt was the richest province in the empire, and its fertile land soon became the principal source of free grain to feed the population of Rome. Augustus's armies also completed the conquest of Spain and made gains in Germany, extending Roman rule as far as the River Danube and the River Rhine. The main difficulty for the Roman army was defending its frontiers. One stretch of the frontier in Germany, between the Danube and Rhine, was particularly hard to patrol. In 9 CE, when three Roman legions marched deep into the Teutoburg Forest on the other side of the River Rhine, they were ambushed by Germanic warriors and totally destroyed. Augustus was so distressed by the news that he refused to cut his hair and beard for several months. It was said that he used to beat his head against a door shouting, "Give me back my legions!" After that he gave up all idea of further conquests in Germany.

PROTECTIVE HEADGEAR
A legionary's helmet was designed to protect the head, cheeks and neck without restricting vision or blocking out sound. The crest was attached for military parades.

ON THE MARCH
A legion of around 5,000 men was split into ten divisions called cohorts. The smallest fighting unit was the century of 80 men.

Augustus was responsible for turning the army into a professional force of career soldiers. He reduced the number of legions and introduced the idea of using auxiliaries – these were soldiers in the provinces, who were given Roman citizenship at the end of their service. Soldiers were not allowed to marry, and they had to stay in the army for 16 years. In return, they were paid well and were often rewarded with gifts. By the end of Augustus's reign, the Roman army numbered more than 300,000 men. He also formed an elite corps of soldiers, known as the Praetorian Guard, to protect him and his family. The guards were normally stationed in Rome and were paid at three times the rate of ordinary soldiers.

Augustus created 28 new colonies in various parts of the empire, where retired soldiers from his legions were given small plots of land to farm. The sons of these veterans followed their fathers into the army, and in the course of time, the provinces in distant parts of the empire began to provide more recruits for the army than the city of Rome itself. These colonies helped to spread the civilized Roman way of life among the local inhabitants.

ELITE TROOPS
Over time, the Praetorian Guard, an elite force of carefully chosen men, came to hold great power in Rome. The guards in this carving are taking part in an imperial parade.

TEMPLE DOORS
This coin shows the doors of the Temple of Janus Quirinus, which were only closed in times of peace.

LASTING STEPS
Augustus built the massive Temple of Mars in the heart of his Forum. A marble flight of steps is all that now remains.

During his long reign, Augustus visited nearly every part of his empire. He placed his legions carefully so that he could move them rapidly to end rebellions or invasions. He won the support of local leaders, and imposed Roman law and order upon even the most distant provinces. But he was also willing to depose rulers whom he did not consider suitable or loyal.

CITY OF MARBLE
Augustus and his successors turned Rome into a magnificent city of temples, basilicas and theatres.

Under Augustus's rule, peace and prosperity returned to Rome. Times of peace were marked by the closing of the doors of a certain temple, known as the temple of Janus Quirinus. During the rule of Augustus, the doors were shut three times. Peace and good order were not the only benefits of Roman rule. One of Augustus's greatest achievements was the rebuilding of the city of Rome. It was his proud claim that he found the city made of bricks and left it clad in marble. He built a new Forum, as well as three great temples to Mars, Jupiter and Apollo. He boasted that, in a single year, he had erected or restored 82 temples. This was not an act of piety on his part, but a statement of his power. The emperor's image was everywhere – on coins, on statues and in paintings. He used his own funds to build basilicas and theatres, and urged wealthy Romans to pay for other public projects. He started a fire service (fire was a

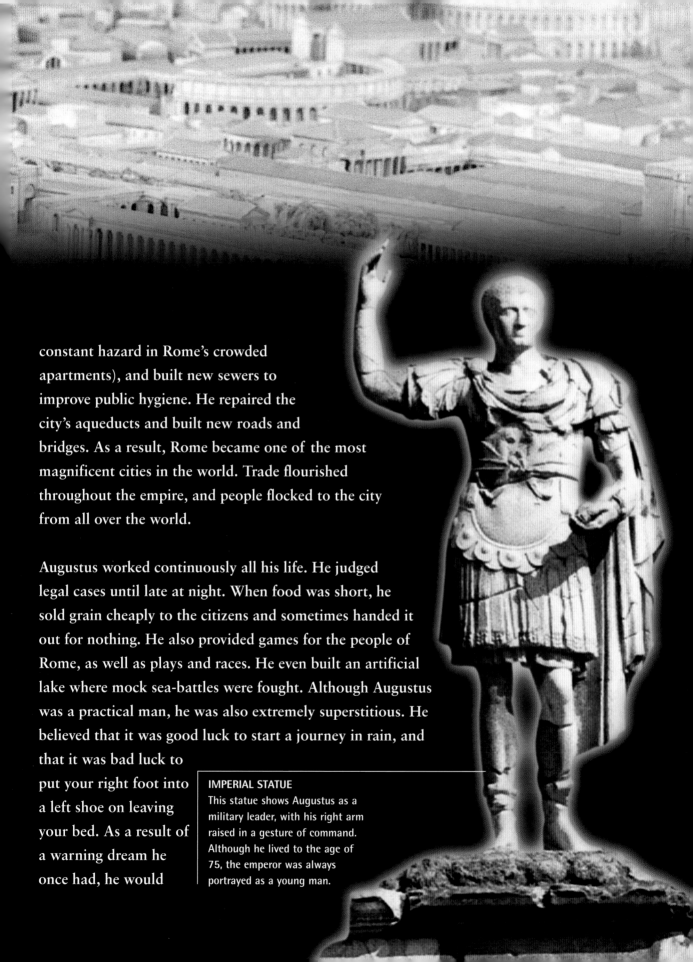

constant hazard in Rome's crowded apartments), and built new sewers to improve public hygiene. He repaired the city's aqueducts and built new roads and bridges. As a result, Rome became one of the most magnificent cities in the world. Trade flourished throughout the empire, and people flocked to the city from all over the world.

Augustus worked continuously all his life. He judged legal cases until late at night. When food was short, he sold grain cheaply to the citizens and sometimes handed it out for nothing. He also provided games for the people of Rome, as well as plays and races. He even built an artificial lake where mock sea-battles were fought. Although Augustus was a practical man, he was also extremely superstitious. He believed that it was good luck to start a journey in rain, and that it was bad luck to put your right foot into a left shoe on leaving your bed. As a result of a warning dream he once had, he would

IMPERIAL STATUE
This statue shows Augustus as a military leader, with his right arm raised in a gesture of command. Although he lived to the age of 75, the emperor was always portrayed as a young man.

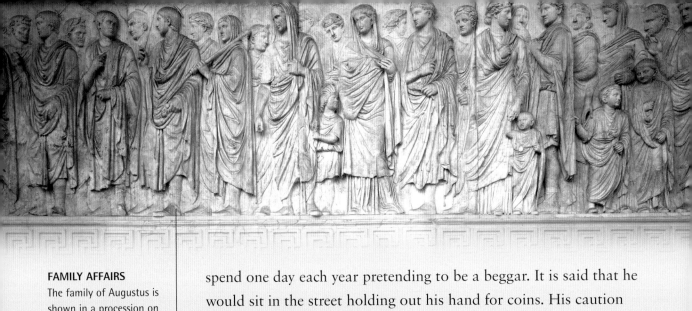

FAMILY AFFAIRS

The family of Augustus is shown in a procession on this carved frieze from the *Ara Pacis* (Altar of Peace). Augustus built this monument to celebrate the end of the civil war.

ISLAND RETREAT

Tiberius built a luxurious villa for himself on top of a cliff on the rocky island of Capri. He lived there in seclusion, far from the cares of government.

spend one day each year pretending to be a beggar. It is said that he would sit in the street holding out his hand for coins. His caution seems to have paid off. Augustus did not die until he was 75, which was an advanced age by Roman standards. He had created a political system that lasted for many generations, and defined the scale of the empire for the next 250 years. Though his successors might add to the empire from time to time, little was ever lost.

Augustus and his wife Livia had no children, although Livia had a son, Tiberius, from a previous marriage. Augustus named Tiberius as his heir, so creating a system whereby power passed on the death of the emperor to another member of his family. This is known as dynastic rule, and the dynasty founded by Augustus is called the Julio-Claudian dynasty. It ruled Rome for 50 years after his death. This system seemed the only way to bring stability to a state that had been plunged into warfare so many times because of the ambition of men hungry for power. But it was perhaps unwise to make birth, rather than ability, the basis for supreme leadership.

Tiberius was 54 when he inherited the role of emperor from Augustus in the summer of 14 CE. He had been a highly successful war commander and had shared supreme power with Augustus for the last two years of the emperor's life. He was not, however, Augustus's first choice of heir. The emperor had been very close to his two grandsons, Gaius and Lucius, and had adopted them as his own children. Both Gaius and Lucius had died as young men, and there were rumours that Tiberius's mother, Livia, had killed off all the other heirs, leaving Tiberius as the only successor.

It seems that Tiberius was reluctant to accept the title of emperor. He often used to say that having supreme power in Rome was like "holding a wolf by the ears". He was a stern and forbidding man. One of his most famous expressions was, "Let them hate me, as long as they respect me." However, he despised flatterers and disliked being called *dominus*, or "my lord". When one magistrate tried to embrace his knees, Tiberius retreated so rapidly that he fell backwards.

GLOOMY EMPEROR
Tiberius had already retired from public life when he was called to Rome to become emperor. He was an unpopular ruler, who was portrayed by the historian Suetonius as a mean-spirited tyrant.

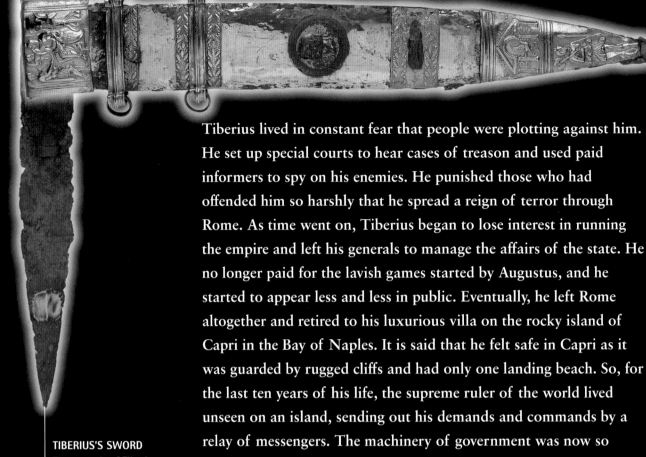

Tiberius lived in constant fear that people were plotting against him. He set up special courts to hear cases of treason and used paid informers to spy on his enemies. He punished those who had offended him so harshly that he spread a reign of terror through Rome. As time went on, Tiberius began to lose interest in running the empire and left his generals to manage the affairs of the state. He no longer paid for the lavish games started by Augustus, and he started to appear less and less in public. Eventually, he left Rome altogether and retired to his luxurious villa on the rocky island of Capri in the Bay of Naples. It is said that he felt safe in Capri as it was guarded by rugged cliffs and had only one landing beach. So, for the last ten years of his life, the supreme ruler of the world lived unseen on an island, sending out his demands and commands by a relay of messengers. The machinery of government was now so efficient that it carried on without him.

It is said that towards the end of his life, Tiberius became cruel and vindictive, ordering punishments and killings on a regular basis. There was a spot in Capri where his victims were tortured and then thrown off the cliff into the sea. When the news of his death came in 37 CE, after 22 years of supreme rule, the people of Rome ran joyfully into the streets exclaiming, "Into the Tiber with Tiberius!"

Tiberius was succeeded by his grandson, Gaius, who was known as Caligula, a name meaning "little boots". Caligula's father Germanicus had been a famous general, and when Caligula was a young boy, he dressed like a Roman soldier in a tunic and miniature boots. Caligula's mother and two of his brothers had died in prison, victims of Tiberius's reign of terror. Caligula's own chances of survival did not look promising. But, when Caligula was 18, Tiberius invited him to the island of Capri and made him his heir.

TIBERIUS'S SWORD
The portrait of Tiberius on the scabbard of this fine sword suggests that it may have been a gift from him to one of his senior officers.

LITTLE BOOTS
Caligula owed his nickname to a miniature pair of boots like these. Military sandals, called *caligae*, were strong, well ventilated and designed for marching.

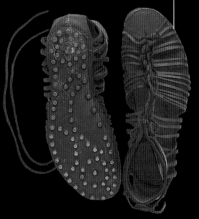

It was rumoured that Caligula tried to hasten Tiberius's end by having him smothered with a pillow. Certainly the people of Rome greeted their new emperor with joy. He was a young man of 25, and the son of a hero. After the suspicious and bloody reign of Tiberius, they thought he could only be an improvement. In fact, he would prove them wrong – he was far worse.

At first Caligula seemed to be a good and just emperor. He allowed those who had been sent into exile by Tiberius to return to Rome, and he pardoned those facing criminal charges. He seemed to have a greater interest in the business of government than Tiberius, and he showed his generosity to the Roman people by handing out gold pieces and bringing back lavish games and public entertainments. In the early days of his reign, he was trying to prove that he was quite a different emperor from the unpopular Tiberius.

Suetonius, the historian

Many famous stories of the early emperors are told by a historian named Suetonius, who wrote *Lives of the Twelve Caesars* – an account of the Roman rulers from Caesar to Domitian. According to Suetonius, Caligula kept his favourite racehorse, Incitatus, in a marble stall and tried to make the horse a consul as a deliberate insult to the Senate.

Purple was the colour worn by emperors.

CALIGULA
When Tiberius chose Caligula as his heir, he boasted that "he was rearing a viper for the Roman people". This portrait of Caligula probably flatters him. According to Suetonius, Caligula was bald and rather ugly.

GUARD CAMP
This coin shows the camp of the Praetorian Guard where Claudius was taken to be proclaimed emperor.

It was not long before Caligula showed that he had a darker and more vicious character than his grandfather. Declaring that he was a living god, he built a golden shrine containing a life-sized statue of himself. It is said that he had whispered conversations with the statue of Jupiter in the temple on the Capitol, and carried a golden image of a thunderbolt, the emblem of Jupiter. Towards the end of his reign, he travelled round Rome dressed in women's clothes, encrusted with jewels. These antics may have been dreamed up to impress his power on the Roman people – or he may simply have been insane.

Caligula's cruelty was as great as his vanity. One of his most famous sayings was, "Remember that I can do anything I want to anybody." He loved games and shows of all kinds, and imported hundreds of wild beasts to be hunted down in the arena. When butchers' meat became too expensive to feed all the

SURPRISE CHOICE
Fearing for his life, Claudius was said to be hiding behind a curtain in the imperial palace when the Praetorian Guard found him and proclaimed him emperor.

wild animals, it is said that he fed them convicts. The people of
Rome came to hate and fear him. In 41 CE, after ruling for less than
four years, Caligula was stabbed more than 30 times by the
commanders of the Praetorian Guard. At the age of 29, the monster
of Rome was dead.

After the death of Caligula, there was much confusion in Rome and
in the imperial palace. The Praetorian Guard feared that the Senate,
appalled by Caligula's deeds, would take steps to restore the Roman
Republic. If that happened, the guards would no longer have a patron
and a place in Rome. So when they found Caligula's uncle, Claudius,
hiding in terror in the palace, they took him to their camp and
declared him emperor.

Claudius appears to have had some
kind of disability. He stammered
and had a weakness in his legs,
which impaired his walking.
Some people doubted that he
would be capable of ruling.
In fact, he was a clever
man and a good
emperor.

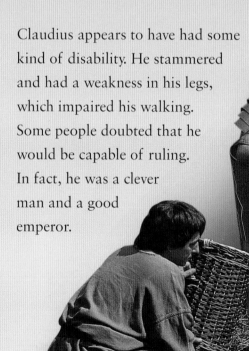

ROMAN BRITAIN
The Roman conquest of
Britain, started by Claudius
in 43 CE, took more than
40 years to complete.
Throughout this time, the
Romans were never able to
subdue the warlike tribes
of Scotland.

Claudius might have been a nervous man – he was afraid of being assassinated and had everyone coming into his presence searched for weapons – but he showed some ability as emperor. Caligula had let the empire fall into disarray. Claudius ruled with the help of a council of ministers. He was the first emperor to invite citizens from the provinces to become senators. He built aqueducts to bring fresh water to Rome and increased the supply of grain. He was also a hard-working judge who heard cases in the law courts every day.

His main achievement was the invasion and conquest of a remote island on the fringe of an empire known as Britain. In 43 CE, his generals fought a hard campaign against a number of tribes in the south of Britain, while Claudius waited in Gaul. Once it was safe to do so, he crossed to Britain and joined his army for its final victorious advance on the enemy capital, Camulodunum (Colchester). On his return, he announced that he had truly made Rome master of the entire world.

His success abroad did not leave him safe at home, however. His own wife, Messallina, hatched a plot to murder him, but Claudius heard of the plan, and had her executed. He married again, even more disastrously. His new wife, Agrippina, is supposed to have killed him by sprinkling poison on his favourite dish of mushrooms. After Claudius's death, in 54 CE, Agrippina's 16-year-old son, Nero, was declared emperor. The private lives of the emperors were awash with blood, especially the blood of those closest to them.

SCHEMING WIFE
Claudius married his fourth wife Agrippina in 49 CE. As they were uncle and niece, they needed special permission to marry from the Senate. Agrippina schemed to make her son Nero emperor rather than Claudius's son Britannicus.

DEADLY DISH
Poison was sprinkled on the mushrooms by the traitorous palace taster, Halotus. Agrippina put a second dose of poison on a feather that Claudius was using to help him vomit.

Agrippina was the sister of Caligula. She was devoted to Nero and had persuaded Claudius to make him his heir, although he had a son of his own. Yet less than a year after Nero became emperor, he dismissed his mother from the palace. Four years later, he arranged her death by faking an accident at sea. That done, Nero gave himself up entirely to his private pleasures, whether music or singing, painting or horse-racing, literature or gymnastics. Nero was convinced he had a beautiful voice. He took part in music festivals and of course won all the prizes. He sang in various plays and would often perform for hours on end. It was said that members of the audience would climb over the walls of the theatre to escape, or even pretend to be dead so that they could be carried out of the audience.

After the murder of his mother, Nero started his own reign of terror against his enemies and rivals. He condemned many rich Romans to death for treason and then seized their property.

SECRET MEETINGS
Nero was ruthless in his persecution of the Christians and accused them of starting the Great Fire of Rome in 64 CE. Christians were forced to meet in secret in the catacombs, the old underground burial chambers in Rome.

He ordered many of his victims to commit suicide by slitting their wrists. That at least was a noble and relatively painless death, compared to being crucified or thrown to the wild beasts in the arena.

In 64 CE, a great fire spread through much of Rome and destroyed many streets and buildings. Rumours grew that Nero had set fire to the city himself so that he could build a country mansion on the land. It was also said that he performed a song to the tune of a lyre while Rome burned. This story is unlikely to be true. But when the Roman people looked for someone to blame, Nero accused the followers of a new religion, Christianity, of having started the fire. In a wave of persecutions, he had many Christians crucified, putting them on great crosses in his garden, and then setting them alight as human torches.

After the fire, Nero built a luxurious palace in the centre of Rome. The Domus Aurea, or Golden House, stood in a park that stretched over 50 hectares (125 acres) of woods, lake and gardens. In the entrance court, he raised a giant statue of himself, some 36 m (120 feet) in height. The palace walls were covered with gold and studded with precious stones. The ceilings

LIFE OF A MONSTER
Nero is remembered as a man who tortured and killed his opponents and burned down Rome for his own ends. But for the first five years of his reign he was a popular ruler in Rome.

DAY AT THE RACES
The early emperors shared the people's passion for racing. This terracotta plaque shows a charioteer driving his team of horses in a race.

could be pulled back to allow a gentle rain of flowers or perfume, while the roof of the main dining room was painted like the sky, and is said to have revolved slowly above the diners.

In the spring of 68 CE, some legions in Spain rose up in protest against Nero and proclaimed a man named Galba emperor in his place. At the beginning of June, the Senate in Rome also gave their support to Galba. Nero planned to flee the city, but it was too late. As the soldiers came to the palace to arrest him, he stabbed himself in the throat. Before he died, he is supposed to have muttered, "Dead! How great an artist dies with me!" With the fall of Nero, the Julio-Claudian dynasty of emperors came to an end.

THE GOLDEN PALACE
Nero's contemporaries were astounded by the size and splendour of the sprawling palace he built for himself in the centre of Rome. This ceiling fresco from one of the rooms in the Golden House depicts the Greek hero Achilles.

CHAPTER SIX

The shadow of · Vesuvius

After the death of Nero, Rome entered a period of chaos. In 69 CE, Rome was ruled by no fewer than four emperors in a single year and once again faced the turmoil of civil war. It was the accession of Vespasian that brought stability back to the empire.

GALBA WAS ALMOST 70 years old when he succeeded Nero as emperor. He had commanded the army in Germany before becoming governor of a Spanish province. Known for his severity and his greed, he was unpopular with the Roman people. His reign lasted just six months before he was murdered and replaced by his rival Otho (a former companion of Nero). Otho did not survive long either. The armies in Germany had already declared their commander, Vitellius, emperor and were marching towards Rome. Vitellius defeated Otho in battle in April 69 CE, and so became the fourth emperor of this extraordinary year.

News of the chaos in Rome had reached Vespasian, an experienced general who had served loyally in many parts of the empire. In 67 CE, Nero had sent Vespasian to Judaea

◄ The excavated streets of Pompeii

VESPASIAN
This statue of Vespasian conveys his forceful and determined character. He was described by the historian Suetonius as a vigorous man of action with endless energy.

(modern-day Israel) to put down a revolt of the Jews. Vespasian was about to capture Jerusalem, when he heard that chaos had broken out in Rome. He left his son Titus in charge of the Jewish revolt and travelled to Alexandria in Egypt to prevent grain supplies from reaching Rome. In this way, he hoped to force Vitellius to give up his claim to the empire. Several other army commanders supported Vespasian's bid for power and marched on Rome. Vitellius realized his defeat was imminent. As he tried to flee the city, he was dragged off by the soldiers and the mob. He was tortured to death, and his body was thrown into the River Tiber.

Vespasian stayed on in Egypt for almost a year, while his son Titus laid siege to Jerusalem. The city fell in September 70 CE, and Vespasian entered Rome as emperor a month later. He had already named Titus as his fellow consul and chosen heir. When Titus reached Rome the following year, father and son built a magnificent triumphal arch to celebrate the victory over the Jews.

Vespasian did not come from an aristocratic family, but he proved that ability was more important than noble

SIEGE OF MASADA
Jewish rebels in the cliff-top fortress of Masada resisted the Romans for four years. In 74 CE, Roman legionaries built a massive ramp and finally took the fortress by storm.

birth. He managed to bring
calm back to Rome and left the
empire in sound shape for his
successor. He was perhaps the first
emperor since Augustus who was truly
fit for the role. Vespasian's family name
was Flavius, and the dynasty of emperors he
founded is known as the Flavian dynasty. It
lasted for some 30 years.

By now, the principal decisions of government were no
longer taken in the Senate, but in the imperial court.
Everyone with a grievance or a demand flocked there.
Vespasian began his day early, listening to the reports
of his secretaries and officials before greeting those

BOOTY OF WAR
This carved relief from
the Arch of Titus in the
Forum shows Roman
soldiers carrying the
menorah (the seven-
branched candlestick
sacred to the Jews)
through the streets of
Rome in triumph.

PUBLIC LAVATORIES
Many cities built public lavatories like these. Water flowing past in a channel under the seats carried the waste to the sewer.

who had come to consult him. When Vespasian took control of the empire, he discovered that the imperial treasury was almost empty, partly because Nero had spent so wildly during the last years of his reign. To raise funds, Vespasian increased taxes and extorted large sums of money from rich Roman citizens. With this money, Vespasian was able to restore many temples in Rome. He also began to build the Colosseum, a magnificent stone amphitheatre used for gladiator fights and animal hunts.

Unlike many of his predecessors, Vespasian was straightforward and honest, and kept a sense of humour. When Titus complained that a tax Vespasian had put on public lavatories was beneath the dignity of the emperor, he handed him a coin from the first day's takings and asked if it smelled bad. The Romans believed that emperors became gods after death, and when he was dying, Vespasian is said to have muttered, "Oh dear, I think that I am turning into a god." He then struggled to his feet, declaring that a Roman emperor should die standing up.

Vespasian had ruled for ten years. Two months after his son Titus became emperor, there occurred one of the most celebrated, and most terrible, events of the ancient world. On 24 August 79 CE, Mount Vesuvius, a volcano that had been quiet since prehistoric times, erupted without warning, totally destroying the city of Pompeii and two other towns close by.

BUILT TO LAST
The Colosseum took less than ten years to build, and was opened by Titus in 80 CE. To protect spectators from the sun, a huge canvas awning was drawn across the top of the stadium by a team of 1,000 men.

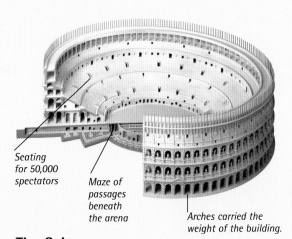

Seating for 50,000 spectators

Maze of passages beneath the arena

Arches carried the weight of the building.

The Colosseum

Dedicated to bloodshed and killing, the Colosseum was where the Romans came to watch gladiators fighting to the death and wild animals being hunted and killed in their thousands. The floor of the arena was covered in sand to soak up the blood of the victims. Beneath it was a maze of machinery, corridors and cells, where the animals were kept in cages. When it was time to fight, the cages were winched up, and the animals were released through trapdoors into the arena. At the end of the day's slaughter, the crowds left through the 80 *vomitoria*, or arched exits on the ground floor.

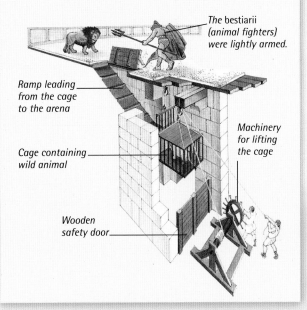

The *bestiarii* (animal fighters) were lightly armed.

Ramp leading from the cage to the arena

Machinery for lifting the cage

Cage containing wild animal

Wooden safety door

FINAL AGONY
This twisted body cast taken of a dog shows that the animal suffered a painful death. Body casts were made by pouring plaster into the hollow spaces left by the bodies of the victims.

END OF POMPEII
Citizens fled in panic as the deadly cloud of ash and pumice rained down upon the city. Although fires broke out, they were soon put out by the ash falling from the sky.

The disaster came suddenly and quickly. Early that morning, there had been a single short outpouring of steam and smoke. At one o'clock in the afternoon, the inferno began. From a distance, it looked like a cloud had come out of the mountain, blotchy, red, black and white. Those who went closer were struck down by burning hot ashes and clumps of pumice. Day had turned to night and, in the darkness, sheets of flame could be seen streaming from the mountain. Ash and pumice were being blasted out at a speed of 996 kph (620 mph). The column of volcanic debris rose until it towered 32 km (20 miles) into the air.

The burning matter rained down ever faster and stronger, the stones and pumice smashing to the ground. An avalanche of boiling mud, gas and molten rock careered down the slopes of the mountain towards the nearby town of Herculaneum. Hundreds of people were fleeing when the avalanche hit them. They were killed instantly. Their bones snapped in half, and their teeth disintegrated in the heat. By the next day, the

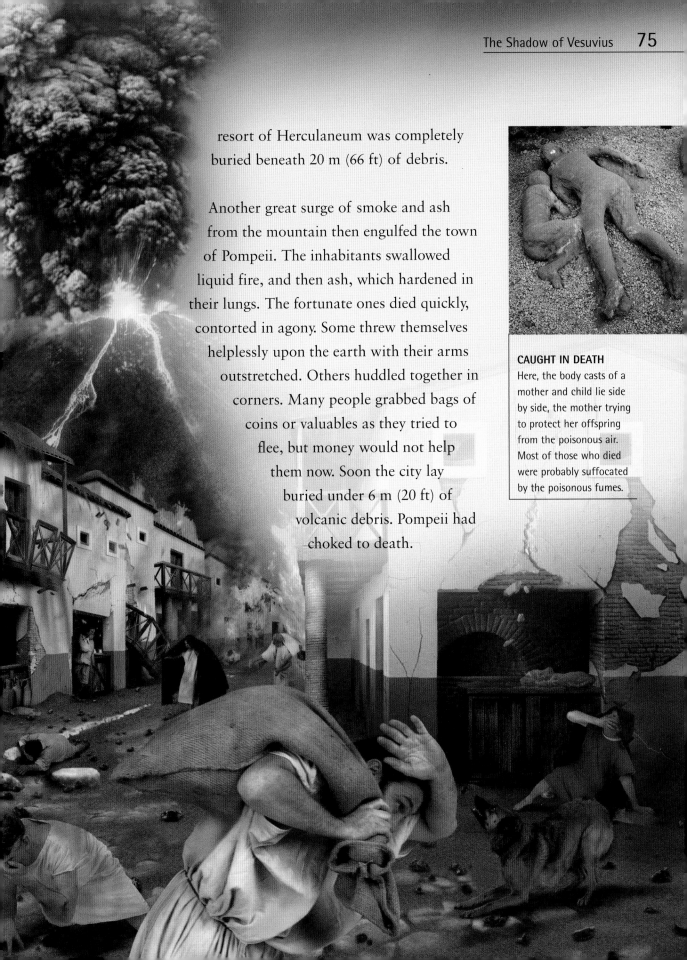

resort of Herculaneum was completely buried beneath 20 m (66 ft) of debris.

Another great surge of smoke and ash from the mountain then engulfed the town of Pompeii. The inhabitants swallowed liquid fire, and then ash, which hardened in their lungs. The fortunate ones died quickly, contorted in agony. Some threw themselves helplessly upon the earth with their arms outstretched. Others huddled together in corners. Many people grabbed bags of coins or valuables as they tried to flee, but money would not help them now. Soon the city lay buried under 6 m (20 ft) of volcanic debris. Pompeii had choked to death.

CAUGHT IN DEATH
Here, the body casts of a mother and child lie side by side, the mother trying to protect her offspring from the poisonous air. Most of those who died were probably suffocated by the poisonous fumes.

ROMAN AMPHITHEATRE
Mount Vesuvius, peaceful today, makes a dramatic backdrop to the amphitheatre at Pompeii. This magnificent arena could seat up to 20,000 spectators.

BURIED IN TIME
Archaeologists had to dig through layers of ash up to 5 m (16 ft) deep to find Pompeii's buried past. The paved forum, pictured here, was once crowded with people and traffic.

Only a few hours before, Pompeii had been an extremely crowded and bustling town on the bay of Naples. On the day of the eruption, many of the town's 20,000 inhabitants escaped, running through the rain of ash. By the next day, the 2,000 people who stayed had all perished. Centuries later, when archaeologists began to excavate, they found a city caught in time. Beneath the layers, they found a forum with temples and basilicas. There were theatres for plays and for music. There were exercise areas for sports and games, and no fewer than five bathhouses. Pompeii had been a thriving trading centre, with a central market place and various colonnaded halls that housed the fish, meat and wool markets. Workshops and taverns lined the paved streets, together with dozens of small shops, selling bread, fruit or vegetables. There was even an aqueduct that brought fresh water into Pompeii and fed the town's public fountains.

Many buildings carried posters advertising forthcoming games or naming the magistrates due for election. People had scrawled slogans and graffiti commenting on the local gladiators and singers. For example, the fans of an actor called Paris had left messages to each other saying things like "Paris is the jewel of the stage" or "Paris, the sweet one". It is interesting to note that the ordinary citizens of a small Italian town like Pompeii were able to read and write. It is a fact that all citizens who joined the Roman army were made to learn Latin, and were also taught to read and write. This helped to spread the Latin language, and a basic knowledge of reading and writing, around the known world.

The name of the emperor Titus is now all but forgotten, but the name of Pompeii lives on in the memory of the world. Titus reigned for a little over two years, and so it is hard to assess his ability as emperor, but he seems to have been popular and capable. He could be cruel and brutal, but he had a high sense of duty. He said on becoming emperor that he would not cause the death of any citizen, and he seems to have been true to his word. On the news of his death the whole of Rome went into mourning.

A VARIED DIET
Fossils such as these eggs found at Pompeii can tell us a lot about the health and diet of the Romans. Bread, olives, nuts and figs were also found the site.

EDUCATED COUPLE
In this portrait, the woman carries a wax tablet, while the man is holding a papyrus scroll. Sheets of papyrus were usually used for important or official documents.

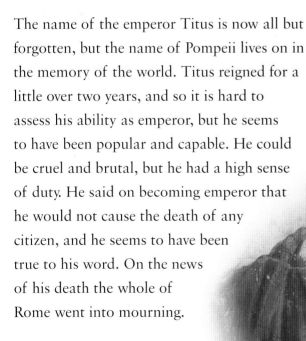

Before he died Titus is reported to have said "I have made only one mistake." No one knows quite what he meant, but he may have regretted naming his younger brother, Domitian, as his successor. Domitian proved once again that dynastic rule was a flawed system of government. He had neither the wisdom of his father, nor the experience of his brother.

TITUS
This coin bears the image of Emperor Titus. He visited Pompeii twice after the eruption, and organized help for the stricken town.

DOMITIAN'S PALACE
Engineers levelled the top of the Palatine Hill to provide the site for Domitian's new palace, shown with its curved facade in this reconstructed model of imperial Rome.

Domitian was determined to print his own personality upon the empire. At first, he tried to buy popularity by funding lavish public games for the people of Rome. He also won the support of the army by raising soldiers' pay. He built and restored more buildings in Rome than any emperor since Augustus, and constructed a magnificent new palace for himself on the Palatine Hill. Monuments and statues bearing his image were erected throughout the empire. All this was paid for by extorting more money from rich citizens and from other groups within the empire (for example, he levied very high taxes on the Jews). For all his faults, Domitian did not neglect the business of the empire. Indeed, he took some of his duties very seriously. He objected to the behaviour of many Roman citizens and passed new laws to curb loose morals. He became very arrogant and remote towards his subjects, and liked to be addressed as "*dominus et deus*" (lord and god). Although an emperor might be given the title of "*divus*" (divine) when he died, most Romans hated the idea of worshipping a living emperor. It was one reason why Caligula had been so resented.

Domitian's suspicions of those around him brought about his downfall. He ordered the execution of many senators and sent others into exile. He also turned on members of the imperial household. Eventually he was killed by assassins, thought to have been hired by his wife, Domitia. It is said that only the soldiers, whose pay he had improved, mourned his passing. He had reigned for 15 years, and with his death in 95 CE, the Flavian dynasty came to an end.

A SUSPICIOUS TYRANT
Regarded as a tyrannical yet efficient ruler, Domitian became increasingly unpopular. He was brutal in his persecution of Christians and Jews and even executed members of his own family.

CHAPTER SEVEN

The *five* *good* emperors

After Domitian's turbulent reign, the Senate appointed an elderly senator called Nerva as emperor. Nerva was the first of a series of rulers known as the "five good emperors". These fair and wise emperors brought stability back to the empire.

NERVA WAS A PATIENT and generous ruler, who came to power at the age of 61. Childless, and elderly by Roman standards, he was the first emperor to select and adopt his successor rather than choose a blood relative. In 97 CE, in a public ceremony on the Capitol, he adopted a popular hero called Trajan as his son. Trajan had the support of both the army and the people. He was the commander of the three legions in Upper Germany and was known for his courage and loyalty. He had been born in the Roman town of Italica in southern Spain and was in his mid-forties at the time of his accession. When Nerva died of a fever, after only two years as emperor, Trajan was ready to take power. But he did not hurry to Rome. Instead, he remained in Germany, visiting the frontiers and inspecting his troops. It was nearly two years before he finally entered Rome.

◄ The dome of the Pantheon in Rome

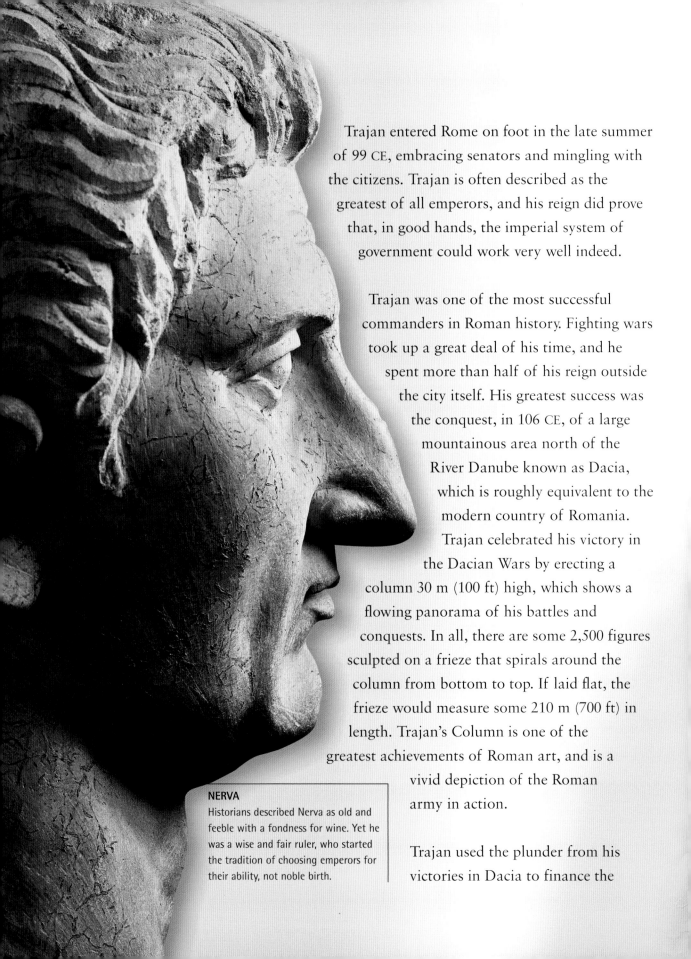

Trajan entered Rome on foot in the late summer of 99 CE, embracing senators and mingling with the citizens. Trajan is often described as the greatest of all emperors, and his reign did prove that, in good hands, the imperial system of government could work very well indeed.

Trajan was one of the most successful commanders in Roman history. Fighting wars took up a great deal of his time, and he spent more than half of his reign outside the city itself. His greatest success was the conquest, in 106 CE, of a large mountainous area north of the River Danube known as Dacia, which is roughly equivalent to the modern country of Romania. Trajan celebrated his victory in the Dacian Wars by erecting a column 30 m (100 ft) high, which shows a flowing panorama of his battles and conquests. In all, there are some 2,500 figures sculpted on a frieze that spirals around the column from bottom to top. If laid flat, the frieze would measure some 210 m (700 ft) in length. Trajan's Column is one of the greatest achievements of Roman art, and is a vivid depiction of the Roman army in action.

Trajan used the plunder from his victories in Dacia to finance the

NERVA
Historians described Nerva as old and feeble with a fondness for wine. Yet he was a wise and fair ruler, who started the tradition of choosing emperors for their ability, not noble birth.

IMPERIAL COIN
This coin shows the emperor Trajan, who was described by the writer Pliny as having a tall stature and noble bearing.

MILITARY MONUMENT
Trajan built this ornate column in 106 CE to commemorate his victory in Dacia. The carved spiral frieze with its scenes of war winds round the column, which still stands in Rome today.

construction of many splendid new buildings in Rome. He commissioned new roads, bridges, canals and towns, and also an enormous forum in Rome, surrounded by markets, libraries and bathhouses. He erected a vast basilica (a public building that housed law courts, shops and offices) that was 85 m (280 ft) long and 24 m (80 ft) wide. The games he staged to celebrate his victories lasted 123 days and involved a total of 10,000 gladiators and 11,000 animals. It was said that under Trajan, the city of Rome recovered the vigour and energy of its early years.

In 114 CE, Trajan set off east on a great campaign to further expand the frontiers of the empire. His goal was Armenia, a kingdom that was sandwiched between the two great empires of Rome and Parthia (Persia). Trajan conquered it and made it into a Roman

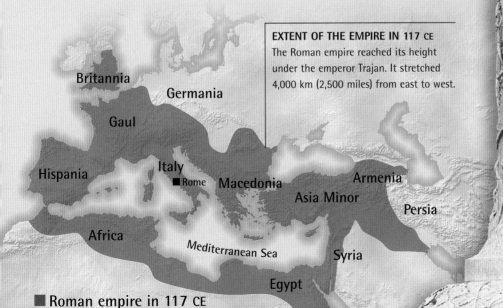

EXTENT OF THE EMPIRE IN 117 CE
The Roman empire reached its height under the emperor Trajan. It stretched 4,000 km (2,500 miles) from east to west.

Britannia

Germania

Gaul

Hispania

Italy
■ Rome

Macedonia

Asia Minor

Armenia

Persia

Africa

Mediterranean Sea

Syria

Egypt

■ **Roman empire in 117 CE**

LEGACY OF A LEADER
Under Hadrian, the Roman world enjoyed 20 years of stable, calm government. Later generations would come to regard his reign as a golden age, the high point of imperial rule.

province. He then marched into Mesopotamia (modern-day Iraq) and took control of the whole country as far as the Persian Gulf. It was an extraordinary achievement, and one that none of his successors was ever able to equal. The truth was, however, that these new territories were too large and too distant for the Romans to control, and many of them were given up in the year of Trajan's death. After reigning for 19 years, Trajan died in 117 CE while on this great military campaign. His ashes were placed in a golden urn at the base of his famous column in Rome.

His successor, Hadrian, was 41 years old. Like Trajan, he came from Italica in Spain. He was the governor of Syria when Trajan died, and the role of emperor seems to have fallen naturally into his hands. He returned to Rome in 118 CE, a year after Trajan's death, and very quickly imposed his will upon the city and the empire. He organized games and gladiatorial contests, and he also began to construct the Pantheon – one of the finest monuments of imperial Rome.

Hadrian believed that the empire had become too vast to control, and he relinquished part of the land that Trajan had conquered. Three years after his arrival in Rome, he set out for his first tour of the empire. It was a journey that lasted four years. He wanted to make sure that his legions were prepared for any conflict that might arise, and that the frontiers were well defended against attacks from barbarian tribes. (The Romans called anyone barbarian who lived outside the bounds of Roman civilization.) He visited Gaul and Germany, and built a great barrier between the River Danube and the River Rhine. This huge defensive structure was 485 km (300 miles) long and was made of earth and timber, topped with a fence of wooden stakes. Hadrian then travelled to northern Britain, where he built a stone wall some 128 km (80 miles) in length to protect the towns and settlements of Roman Britain from the tribes of the country we now call Scotland (the Romans knew it as Caledonia).

The country that Hadrian admired beyond all others was Greece, and he visited the cultural city of Athens on three separate occasions. He had a passion for Greek learning and philosophy and even grew a beard to show his love of all things Greek. Before Hadrian, Roman emperors were usually clean-shaven, and people in Rome associated beards with eastern luxury and weakness until Hadrian made them fashionable.

Hadrian made several more long journeys and visited almost every part of the empire, supervising the armies and strengthening the Roman frontiers. During his reign, he faced only one major uprising – a Jewish revolt in the Middle Eastern province of Judaea.

The Pantheon

Hadrian had originally planned to rebuild Marcus Agrippa's temple of 27 BCE, but the Pantheon was in fact an entirely new structure with a revolutionary design. The entrance porch, with its tall columns and triangular pediment, was in the traditional style, but it led into a spectacular interior – a marble-paved circular chamber that was topped by an enormous dome 43 m (141 ft) in diameter. Hadrian dedicated his new temple to all the gods. The name Pantheon comes from the Greek word *pantheion* (*pan* meaning "all" and *theos* meaning "god").

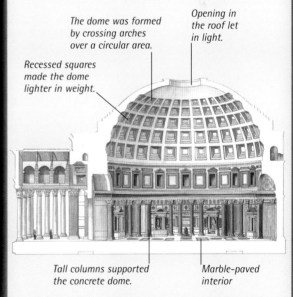

The dome was formed by crossing arches over a circular area.

Opening in the roof let in light.

Recessed squares made the dome lighter in weight.

Tall columns supported the concrete dome.

Marble-paved interior

SACRED SITE
This silver coin, issued by the Jewish leader Simon bar Kochba, shows the sacred Temple in Jerusalem.

In 132 CE, Hadrian attempted to build a temple dedicated to Jupiter on the site of the Temple of Solomon in Jerusalem (the original temple had been destroyed by Titus some 60 years earlier). This was a site sacred to the Jews, who rose in revolt under the leadership of a man named Simon bar Kochba. Hadrian crushed the uprising without pity. Tens of thousands of Jews were killed or enslaved.

During the time he spent in Rome, Hadrian proved to be one of the most hard-working of all the emperors. He introduced laws to deal with tax, marriage and public safety, and he improved the running of

the empire by creating two departments to handle official reports and business. One, for the western half of the empire, used Latin, while the other used Greek, as that was the language spoken by most people in the eastern empire. Hadrian himself supervised the Senate. He met ambassadors from all over the world and was the final judge in legal matters. He presided at the public games and held daily audiences in the imperial palace. But perhaps the happiest moments of his life were spent in his magnificent villa at Tivoli, 24 km (15 miles) from Rome, which included buildings named after the famous places he had visited on his travels.

HADRIAN'S WALL
The stone wall across northern Britain was a bleak posting for the auxiliaries (non-citizen soldiers) who manned the forts along its length. Legionaries moved up to the wall at times of unrest, but for much of its history the frontier was peaceful.

VILLA AT TIVOLI

Hadrian made an amazing replica of Canopus, an Egyptian town, He dug a large canal and imported Egyptian statues to decorate its banks. There were rows of columns joined by alternate arches and graceful caryatids – female figures used as columns.

After a period of ill-health, Hadrian died in 138 CE. Before his death, he named Aurelius Antoninus (who is better known as Antoninus Pius) as his chosen successor. The name "Pius" (meaning dutiful or respectful) seems to have been well deserved. Antoninus Pius was one of the best loved and best tempered of all the Roman emperors. He was apparently modest, unassuming and compassionate. His reign passed without a major war, and he handled the government of the empire so well that almost nothing happened. After a reign of 23 years, he died peacefully in his bed in 161 CE.

His successor was Marcus Aurelius, who ruled at first with his adopted brother Lucius Verus. After Lucius died in 168 CE, Marcus

Aurelius ruled alone for another 11 years. Marcus Aurelius had been well prepared for the duties of emperor. But he always said he would have preferred to study philosophy than run the empire. His journals reveal him to be a thoughtful, solemn and peace-loving man. It was something of an irony that his reign was marked by bitter and almost constant warfare against barbarian tribes.

First, there was a war against the Parthians on the eastern edges of the empire, which arose out of a longstanding dispute over the control of Armenia. Then, several of the German tribes living north of the Danube began to raid across the Roman frontier.

Emperor's palace

Academy (named after Plato's school at Athens).

Tree-lined walkway

Temple of Venus

Greek theatre

Hadrian's villa

This reconstruction shows how Hadrian's villa at Tivoli would have looked during his reign. The buildings sprawled over a wide area, and the grounds were landscaped with shady cypress-lined walkways and sparkling fountains. The villa took ten years to complete and contained many buildings inspired by Hadrian's travels around Greece and Egypt. Among the many wonders was a copy of the Grove of Academe where the Greek philosopher Plato tutored his students.

ANTONINE BATHS
Although these baths in Carthage, North Africa, are named after him, Antoninus Pius did not travel widely. Unlike Hadrian, he was content to rule the empire from Rome.

MARCUS AURELIUS
This elaborate statue of Marcus Aurelius on horseback, made of gilded bronze, is one of the finest works of art to have survived from imperial Rome.

These invasions were part of a large movement of tribes in the vast regions beyond the northern limits of the Roman empire. Tribe pressed against tribe, clan advanced against clan, all setting up an overwhelming pressure on the boundaries of the empire itself.

The empire had enjoyed a long period of peace and stability under Hadrian and Antoninus Pius, but now it was being sorely tested. With admirable patience and

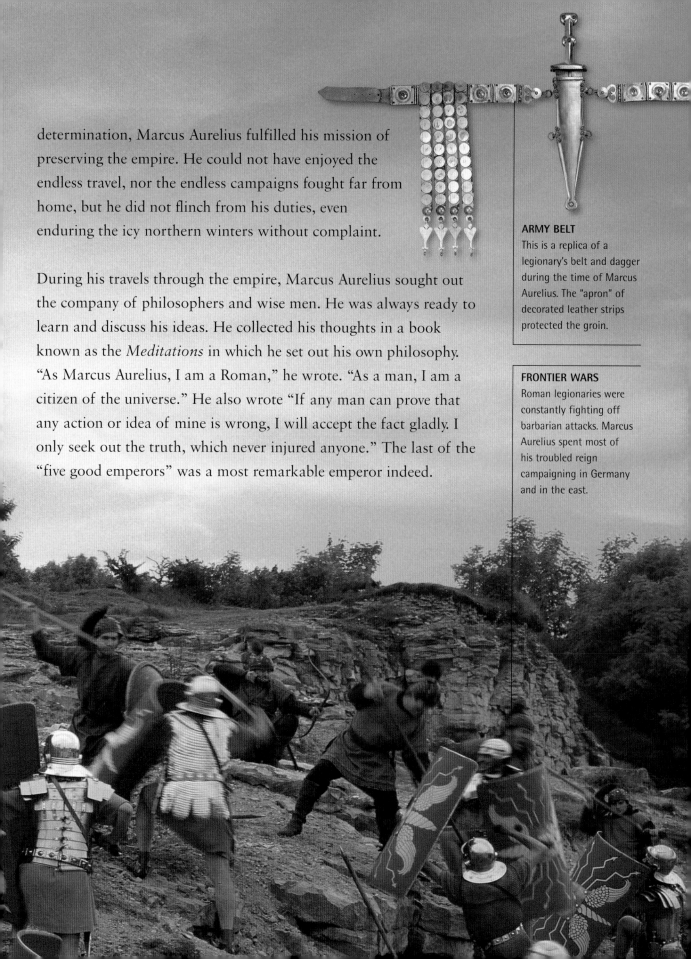

determination, Marcus Aurelius fulfilled his mission of preserving the empire. He could not have enjoyed the endless travel, nor the endless campaigns fought far from home, but he did not flinch from his duties, even enduring the icy northern winters without complaint.

During his travels through the empire, Marcus Aurelius sought out the company of philosophers and wise men. He was always ready to learn and discuss his ideas. He collected his thoughts in a book known as the *Meditations* in which he set out his own philosophy. "As Marcus Aurelius, I am a Roman," he wrote. "As a man, I am a citizen of the universe." He also wrote "If any man can prove that any action or idea of mine is wrong, I will accept the fact gladly. I only seek out the truth, which never injured anyone." The last of the "five good emperors" was a most remarkable emperor indeed.

ARMY BELT
This is a replica of a legionary's belt and dagger during the time of Marcus Aurelius. The "apron" of decorated leather strips protected the groin.

FRONTIER WARS
Roman legionaries were constantly fighting off barbarian attacks. Marcus Aurelius spent most of his troubled reign campaigning in Germany and in the east.

CHAPTER EIGHT

The daily life *of* Rome

Rome enjoyed nearly a century of peace and stability under the five good emperors. By this stage, the city had grown very large, and its population of more than one million came from all parts of the empire. Rich and poor lived almost side by side.

To THE MODERN EYE, ancient Rome would seem squalid, noisy and dirty. Its labyrinth of small, dark streets was packed with people jostling for space. Often streets were full of waste, which people had thrown out of the windows. Yet, at the same time, Rome was the richest and most glorious of all cities. The Romans believed in the architecture of power, and the emperors built on a massive scale. Great arches and triumphal columns were erected to celebrate Roman victories across the empire. The biggest of everything was found in Rome – the biggest amphitheatres, the biggest public baths and the biggest basilicas. One of the ten great aqueducts that brought water to Rome was 64 km (40 miles) long. Roman monuments were built to last in concrete and granite, and many of these impressive buildings are still standing today.

◄ A busy street-scene in Rome

Roman dress

Only Roman citizens had the right to wear a toga, a straight piece of heavy woollen cloth that was wrapped round the body to hang in complicated folds over the shoulder. It was worn over a knee-length tunic, which was the usual form of everyday dress for men. Women wore a long tunic made of wool or linen, and with it a shawl, or *palla*. Both men and women wore cloaks fastened at the shoulder with a brooch called a *fibula*.

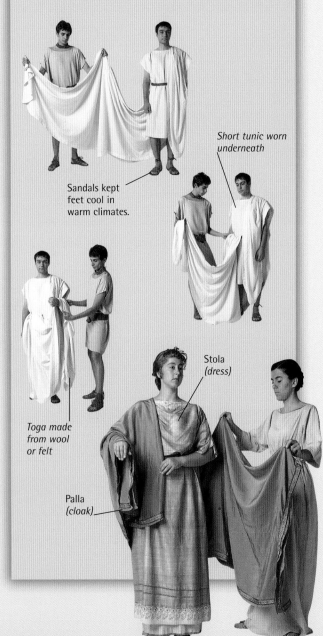

Sandals kept feet cool in warm climates.

Short tunic worn underneath

Toga made from wool or felt

Stola (dress)

Palla (cloak)

Money was the path to power and influence in the city, although the old division of patricians and plebeians still existed. The Romans were very concerned with individual status and symbols of rank. Citizens were divided into three groups – the senators, the *equites* (professional men who were descendants of the first Roman cavalry) and the people. Senators wore a broad purple stripe on their togas, while the *equites* had a narrow stripe. Ordinary citizens wore plain white togas. Only the emperor could dress all in purple.

Rank also determined the seating arrangements for theatres and public entertainments. The front seats were reserved for senators and for foreign guests of the state. Behind them sat the *equites*, then the citizen soldiers. Next came all other freeborn Roman male citizens, divided by age into "senior" and "junior" ranks. Behind them sat the "dishonest" citizens, a category that included debtors and fraudsters. Lowest of all came freed slaves, women and gladiators.

Despite their low social ranking, women in Rome had greater freedom than women elsewhere in the ancient world. Freeborn women (those whose parents had not been slaves) were citizens. They did not have all

LIMITED EDUCATION
Women in Rome seldom got more than a basic education. Higher studies were strictly for the men who were groomed for careers in the government.

WEDDING CEREMONY
Most marriages were arranged for financial or political reasons. The wedding usually took place at the bride's house and was witnessed by family and friends. Here, the groom holds a written contract as he clasps his bride's hand to show that they are man and wife. The bride wears a special dress and a bright orange veil.

the rights and duties that men did – for example, they were not allowed to vote – but they had access to the law, and they could inherit and own property. They were considered to be the equal of their husband in family law, and divorces were easily obtained. Roman women may have been excluded from holding public office, but they could still have power and influence. According to historians, women in the imperial and senatorial families were often deeply involved in the world of political scandal and intrigue.

A woman's position in society depended on the status of her husband. Married women spent their time engaged in household tasks, although many had slaves to help them. Widows were able to control their own property. Although most Roman women were not taught to a high standard, a few educated women became teachers and doctors. Some even ran their own successful businesses.

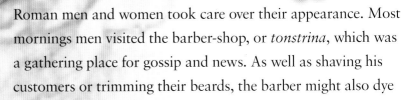

ROMAN FINERY

The jewellery shown here would have belonged to a wealthy woman. These gold dolphin earrings were made for pierced ears and are similar to those worn by women today.

GETTING READY

Fashionable women, attended by slaves, performed a lengthy morning toilet of hairdressing and make-up. In the days of the early Republic, women wore their hair in a simple bun. Later, curls and plaits became the fashion.

Roman men and women took care over their appearance. Most mornings men visited the barber-shop, or *tonstrina*, which was a gathering place for gossip and news. As well as shaving his customers or trimming their beards, the barber might also dye their hair, and would sprinkle them with perfume. Roman women liked to wear jewellery and make-up. Cosmetic cases, brushes and tweezers have been found all over the Roman world, as well as ornate mirrors and hair accessories. Wealthy women took particular trouble with their hair, drawing it back and fastening it in a knot with a jewelled pin or with an ornamental net.

Many Roman women could read and write. They wrote on thin sheets of wood or on waxed tablets, using a sharp stick called a stylus. These tablets, held between hinged wooden boards, were the usual way of sending messages or writing to friends in Rome. Businessmen wrote letters and contracts on sheets of Egyptian papyrus with reed pens.

The family was the fundamental unit of Roman society. The father, or *paterfamilias*, was the head of the household in every sense and held power over his entire family. He was responsible for the education and upbringing of his children. He could punish them however he wished, and could even have them killed. A father was legally permitted to leave a sickly newborn child on a public rubbish dump to die of cold or hunger.

As head of the household, the father's most important duty was to perform the daily rituals that kept the family from harm. These rituals dated back to the earliest days of the Republic. For example, a sacred salted cake was thrown into the fire at the main meal of the day as an offering to Vesta, the goddess of the hearth. Each house had a small shrine called a *lararium*, where offerings were made every morning to the other household gods such as the *lares* and the *penates*.

Many people in imperial Rome thought that the standards of family life had weakened since the days of the Republic, and it became fashionable to complain that "the customs of our ancestors" had been ruined by too much wealth and too much luxury.

GUARDING THE HOME
This is a bronze statue of a *lar* – the spirit of the family's ancestors. *Lares* are represented as boys dressed in belted tunics, with a bowl in one hand and an upraised jug in the other.

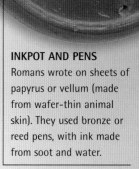

INKPOT AND PENS
Romans wrote on sheets of papyrus or vellum (made from wafer-thin animal skin). They used bronze or reed pens, with ink made from soot and water.

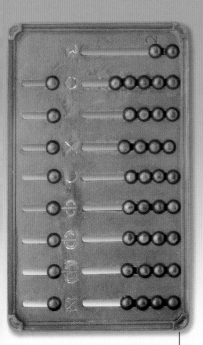

SLAVE TEACHERS
An educated Greek slave copies a letter for his master on papyrus. Parents sometimes had their children taught at home by Greek slaves, a sign of the high value placed on Greek culture and learning.

ROMAN CALCULATOR
The Romans used an abacus for quick arithmetic. A merchant could work out complicated transactions in seconds by sliding the beads along the grooves. Each bead represented a different unit.

From the age of seven to eleven, boys and girls attended a primary school. Girls would then stay at home to learn housework in preparation for marriage, but boys could go on to a grammar school. They were not educated for a specific career, but to take their place in Roman society. Pupils were taught the elements of mathematics and of grammar, and were made to learn poetry by heart to encourage clear speaking. Many boys were taught Greek so that they could read both Greek and Latin literature. If a rich man's son wanted a political or legal career, it was essential for him to learn oratory (the art of public speaking).

Children from poorer families received no schooling at all, but were sent out to make their living, or to supplement the family income, at a very early age.

Although the lifestyles of the ancient Romans depended very much on income, even the poorest citizens of Rome enjoyed the benefits of the state. Every month, the emperor gave the poor people of Rome free handouts of grain called the *annona*. They were also given free entrance to the bathhouses and the public games. The public games were an essential aspect of Roman society. The *ludi* (chariot racing, gladiatorial combats, mock sea-battles and theatrical performances) drew huge crowds, and were staged by emperors or senators in honour of a god or military victory. Hordes of people gathered at the racetrack, called a circus, for a day out. By the 4th century CE, the Roman people were enjoying 175 days of public games a year. No civilization in the world has given so many public holidays to its working people. Roman emperors relied on bread and circuses to keep their people happy.

GAMES OF CHANCE
Roman men loved to gamble and bet on the outcomes of contests. They threw dice and played board games similar to draughts or backgammon, using glass counters.

A BOY'S LIFE
This carving from a sarcophagus shows the stages in a boy's life, from being nursed in his mother's arms to reciting to his father. The middle scene shows him riding his donkey chariot.

One of the most popular forms of entertainment was chariot racing, or *ludi circenses*. The largest racetrack, the Circus Maximus in Rome, had room for 260,000 spectators and was the largest public arena in the world.

Twelve charioteers took part in each race. They belonged to four teams known as the Blues, Reds, Greens and Whites, and each team had its loyal supporters in Rome. Pictures of the most popular and successful charioteers were stuck up on walls all over the city, and many of the leading stars became very rich indeed.

DICING WITH DEATH
The chariots on the racetrack travelled at great speed, and the charioteers needed all their strength and skill to control their horses on the tight bends. Fans went so far as to bury curses beside the track, wishing an accident on a particular charioteer so that their own favourite would win.

RACING CHARIOT
Chariots were lightly built for maximum speed. This is a model of a *quadriga*, pulled by four horses. Similar chariots called *bigae* were pulled by two horses. Charioteers tied the reins around their waists, but carried knives so they could cut themselves free in a crash.

The main draw of the games were the gladiators – armed men who fought savagely in hand-to-hand combat in the amphitheatre. Gladiators were usually prisoners, slaves or criminals. They fought

each other with a variety of weapons – some had swords, shields and helmets, while others had tridents and nets. Before they began their combats, they would parade around the arena and stop in front of the emperor's box. Here they would call out "Hail, Caesar, we who are about to die salute you!"

The crowd bet upon the results of the contests, and roared their approval or their disappointment. When a gladiator fell into the sand, dead or dying, he was finished off by having his head smashed with a mallet. If a gladiator had fought bravely, the crowd would shout for his life to be spared.

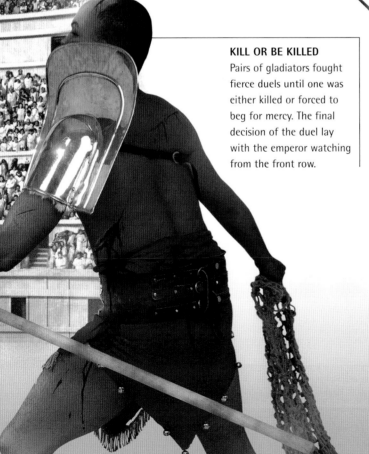

KILL OR BE KILLED
Pairs of gladiators fought fierce duels until one was either killed or forced to beg for mercy. The final decision of the duel lay with the emperor watching from the front row.

Gladiators

There were at least 16 different types of gladiator, ranging from the heavily armed *thrax* who carried a short, curved sword, to the *retiarius*, or net-fighter. Gladiators tended to win their contests by outwitting their opponents, rather than by brute force. They ate a special diet of boiled beans and barley to make them tough. The fight promoters gave their best fighters special names such as *Pugnax* (Picker of Quarrels) or *Tigris* (Tiger).

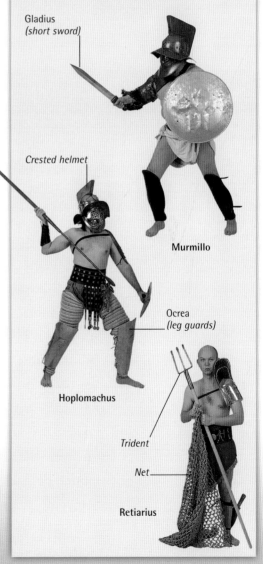

Gladius (short sword)

Crested helmet

Murmillo

Ocrea (leg guards)

Hoplomachus

Trident

Net

Retiarius

PROTECTIVE HELMET
Gladiator armour was designed to look spectacular. This helmet protected the gladiator's head from sword blows, but gave him only limited vision.

There must have been times when the arena was left full of dead bodies, but gladiators were professional fighters, who were trained to please the crowds. While death was always a likely outcome of the combats, it was not inevitable. Victories could bring fame, fortune and freedom from slavery. Many gladiators returned to fight again and again until they were able to retire from the arena as wealthy men. Freed gladiators often set up their own gladiator schools.

BARBARIC SHOWS
Exotic animals were shipped from all over the empire to fight in the arena. In games held by the emperor Trajan to celebrate his Dacian victory, 11,000 wild beasts perished in total.

Many public games were barbaric spectacles. In one of the mock sea-battles beloved by the emperors, 20,000 condemned prisoners from all over the empire were forced to fight one another. This fake sea-battle caused more casualties than any real one. People also flocked to watch the barbaric hunting displays held in the Colosseum. Some 5,000 animals were slaughtered in a single afternoon to celebrate the amphitheatre's opening in 80 CE. The animals were hunted by packs of dogs and by men carrying spears and javelins. The hunters (*venatores*) were often prisoners of war or criminals who had been condemned to death. They normally wore no protective clothing. Exotic animals were in high demand at these shows – lions, tigers, leopards, crocodiles, rhinos, and even ostriches. As a result of the Roman thirst for blood, elephants became extinct in North Africa.

There were many ways for Romans to relax in the city. They could play games, listen to music or go to the theatre. The Romans adopted the idea of theatre from the Greeks. At first, Roman plays tended to be translations of traditional Greek dramas. Later, original plays were written by playwrights such as Plautus and Terence, whose comedies were popular during the 2nd century BCE. Roman audiences generally preferred comedies to tragedies. The first plays were staged in wooden theatres, but these were later replaced by permanent structures built of stone. As theatres were often large, actors wore masks to help the audience recognize the various types of characters. Masks could denote comic and tragic figures, male and female, and young and old. Male characters wore brown masks, whereas female characters wore white. But behind the masks, all the actors were men.

In the afternoons, many Romans went to the public baths, where they washed away the dirt of the city and chatted to friends. The bathhouses opened at midday and were crowded with customers, rich

AT THE THEATRE
This mosaic shows a group of actors preparing for a play. Two actors are practising their dance steps, while another is being helped into his costume. Meanwhile a musician is playing the double pipes.

HOT SPRINGS
The natural hot spring at Bath in Britain was used by the Romans as a medical bathing complex, or healing spa. Sick people came from all over the country to seek a cure by swimming in the waters.

BATH ACCESSORIES
The Romans did not have soap but rubbed their skin with olive oil, which they kept in a flask like the one shown here. They used curved implements called *strigils* to scrape the oil off, and with it came all the dirt and dust of the city.

Heating the bathhouse

Public baths were heated by a system known as a hypocaust. An underground furnace, stoked by slaves, sent hot air under the floors and up through spaces behind special tiles on the walls. To allow the heat to circulate freely, the floors were supported by brick pillars. Water heated in a boiler above the furnace was sent to the baths through pipes.

In the dry hot rooms, the hot air passed underneath the floor and up through cavities in the walls to the chimneys in the roof. The walls and floors became so hot that people had to wear wooden clogs to avoid burning their feet.

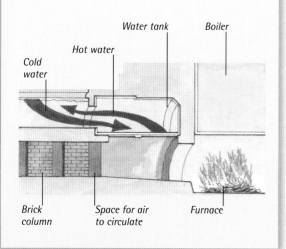

and poor, patricians and plebeians. They were often large and elaborate buildings. At the centre, was the cold room, or *frigidarium*, a lofty marbled hall with cold plunge pools in each corner. Leading out of the *frigidarium* was a series of heated rooms that got steadily hotter and hotter. The heat was either dry, like a sauna, or steamy, like a Turkish bath, and there were hot-water pools for the bathers to plunge in.

Public baths were not just places for washing. They were busy social centres where people could chat, exercise, play games, do business or even have their hair cut or their legs waxed. Men and women normally bathed at separate times, and sometimes in separate areas. Children bathed with the women. On arrival, people undressed and left their clothes in a changing room. They would then move between the rooms, sweating, cooling off and plunging into the pools. The bathers could buy food or hot drinks as they lounged on the marble benches or waited to be massaged by a slave. The baths sometimes included libraries, and there were even exhibitions of art in the elaborately decorated halls. It is estimated that there were over 1,000 bathhouses in Rome, and the largest of them, the Baths of Diocletian, covered an area of 13 hectares (32 acres).

SNACKS ON THE STREET
Romans could buy hot drinks and snacks from take-away shops called *thermopolia*. Snacks were served from the pottery jars set into the counters.

As the crowds hurried home from their daily activities, they passed through streets crowded with shops and markets. There were wine-shops and cook-shops of every description. There were bakers and barbers, cobblers and cloth-dyers, snack shops and spice shops. Shops opened right onto the street and goods were often produced at the back of the building. Outdoor markets sold vegetables, meat, fish and grain. It seems to have been the custom in Rome for the men to shop, rather than the women, although household slaves would have shopped for the wealthier families. Shops opened early and closed late, with a break in the afternoon. At the end of the day, owners shut up their shops by padlocking heavy wooden shutters to the pavement.

Each day, the Romans would make a kind of barley porridge from bread and grain. Other staples included wine and olive oil, used both for lighting and for cooking. From the fruit and vegetable markets came apples, pears, apricots, broad beans, lentils, peas and turnips. Cheese and a fish pickle called *garum* would be bought for the family meals, as well as pork, chicken and rabbit. On special occasions, great efforts would be made to get hold of such delicacies as dormice, snails and small birds.

EATING AT HOME
This elaborate dish of tiny birds, asparagus and quails' eggs would have been served to important guests, perhaps during a feast or banquet. Fish, bread and grapes were more usual fare.

In wealthier households, dinner was a formal meal that started in the late afternoon and lasted all evening. Romans did not sit at a table and chair to dine, but lay on their stomachs or sides on couches and took their food and drink from a low table in front of them. The dinner began with a first course of eggs or seafood and honeyed wine known as the *gustatio*. This was followed by the *prima cena* (main dish) of fish and meat served with vegetables, completed by the *secunda cena* of dessert and fruit. Wine was generally mixed with water. No eating implements were used – diners ate with their hands, and slaves stood by with basins of water and towels. It was a sign of good manners to belch at the end of a meal, and at a full Roman banquet with seven courses, some guests would tickle their throats with a feather to make themselves sick. They could then go back to eating with an empty stomach and a renewed appetite. Between courses, guests were entertained by poets, musicians and magicians.

HOUSE OF THE FAUN
This house at Pompeii is named the House of the Faun after the statue of the dancing faun in the middle of the ornamental pool. This great Roman *domus* (town house) took up an entire *insula* (street block) covering an area of 3,000 sq m (32,000 sq ft).

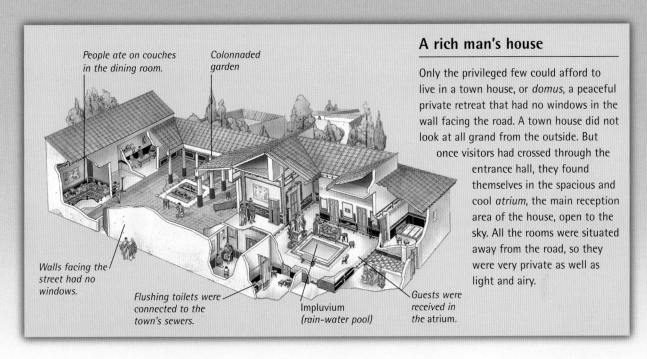

People ate on couches in the dining room.

Colonnaded garden

Walls facing the street had no windows.

Flushing toilets were connected to the town's sewers.

Impluvium (rain-water pool)

Guests were received in the atrium.

A rich man's house

Only the privileged few could afford to live in a town house, or *domus*, a peaceful private retreat that had no windows in the wall facing the road. A town house did not look at all grand from the outside. But once visitors had crossed through the entrance hall, they found themselves in the spacious and cool *atrium*, the main reception area of the house, open to the sky. All the rooms were situated away from the road, so they were very private as well as light and airy.

The grander and more wealthy Romans lived in spacious townhouses that were built around a colonnaded courtyard garden called a *peristylium*, planted with shrubs and flowers. All the rooms of the house opened off the central courtyard. People entered the house through the *vestibulum*, which led through to the main reception area called the *atrium*, where the statues of the household gods were kept. The *atrium* had a central opening in the roof, which let in light and air. The four roofs of the house sloped inwards so that the rain ran off them to fill an *impluvium*, or ornamental pool, in the middle. There was a dining room known as the *triclinium* and various

MOSAIC FLOORS

Interior floors were decorated with mosaics made from small cubes of stone called *tesserae*. Skilled craftworkers worked from drawn plans, pressing tiny pieces of coloured glass or stone into wet plaster to create a picture.

GLASSWARE

An expensive vase like this one made of cameo glass would have had pride of place in the house. White glass was cut away over blue glass to make the pattern.

HEALING HERBS
The Romans knew that many plants had healing qualities. Soldiers were given a daily ration of garlic as a defence against illness.

bedrooms called *cubicula*. A small kitchen contained a sink and an oven, where slaves cooked and prepared the meals. Most wealthy houses had a toilet, which could be flushed with waste water from the kitchen. Houses did not contain much furniture (apart from couches, chairs and tables), but it was elegant and well crafted. The grandest rooms of the house often had elaborate mosaic pictures on the floor and painted ceilings and walls.

So, for the wealthy, living standards were high. But for the poor they were very low. Historians estimate that somewhere between one third and one half of the population depended upon handouts or public charity. The average life expectancy was only 25 years. Of course, many Romans died in infancy or early childhood, and others lived on to old age, but death often came suddenly in the midst of life. Resistance to disease was lowered by malnutrition, and outbreaks of typhus, malaria, cholera or pneumonia would sweep rapidly through the city as a result of bad drains and crowded living conditions.

DOCTOR AND PATIENT
Only the rich could afford doctors. The less wealthy wore charms to ward off disease. If they were sick, they visited a shrine of Aesculapius, the god of healing, to ask for a cure.

The poor people of Rome lived packed together in large apartment blocks known as *insulae*, with little air or light. Shops and workshops on the ground floor looked out onto the street, while each of the floors above (as many as six or seven) was divided into flats. These flats were divided and subdivided to accommodate large numbers of people, and an entire family might live crowded into a single room. There was no heat and no running water. Fresh supplies of water had to be fetched in jars from the nearest public fountain. Most apartments had no toilets, so people used the *foricae*, or public toilets, in the streets. They consisted of a long marble bench with open seats placed above a trench, which was flushed out from time to time with water. Drains carried the sewage and waste from the streets into the River Tiber. The city must have been very smelly, especially in summer or when the river flooded.

Wheeled traffic was forbidden in the city during the day because of overcrowding, so at night the streets of Rome were full of the wagons and carts bringing food and other supplies to the city and taking away the rubbish. The noise made by the rumbling of their wheels was overwhelming, as was the smell of food from the take-away shops mingled with the stink of rubbish thrown into the streets. Away from the main thoroughfares, the unlit streets were dark and often dangerous. All would have been one vast noisy confusion. One Roman poet, Juvenal, remarked that no one should go out to supper without making his will in advance, so great were the risks of being run down by a cart or knifed by a street-robber. Rome must have been a very dangerous place to live indeed.

PUBLIC FOUNTAIN
Thanks to Rome's network of aqueducts, millions of litres of water flowed into the city every day to supply the public fountains and bathhouses.

PACKED TOGETHER
This model shows an apartment block, or *insula*, in which most of Rome's inhabitants lived. They were often badly built and desperately overcrowded. Entire blocks sometimes collapsed under the sheer weight of people.

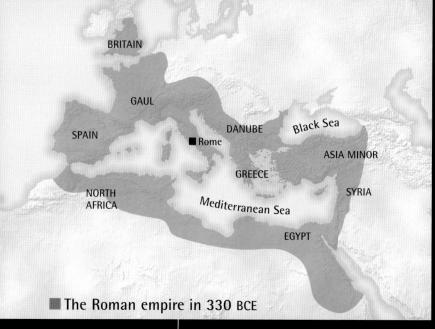

The Roman empire in 330 BCE

THE ROMAN EMPIRE
Between 60 and 80 million people lived within the frontiers of the Roman empire. Every part of the empire was linked to Rome by road, river or sea.

CASH ECONOMY
This frieze shows farm tenants handing over piles of coins as rent. Coins were used throughout the empire, and taxes were paid in cash.

When they conquered a new territory, the Romans built a network of roads to link towns and cities across the province. In the eastern provinces of Syria and Asia Minor, many towns had existed for hundreds of years before the Romans arrived. But in western parts of the empire, such as in Gaul or Britain, new towns grew up around the camps of the Roman legionaries, or at important river or road crossings. Among the great cities of Europe that began in this way are Paris and London, Vienna and Bonn, Budapest and Belgrade.

The new towns were usually built in a grid pattern of paved streets, with forums and basilicas, baths and temples, theatres and aqueducts. The Romans believed they were bringing civilization to a world of barbarians. Wherever possible, they made the local leaders part of the governing system, giving them control over local matters such as maintaining the roads and water supply. Over time, whole

communities were given Roman citizenship, which helped to promote stability and order across the empire. Any man who served in the Roman army became a citizen at the end of his service. Eventually, in 212 CE, a grant was made extending citizenship to all free men and women throughout the empire.

At its height, the empire consisted of an assembly of largely self-governing territories. Latin was used as the official language of government, and many provinces adopted Roman law and customs. Although the lives of the peasants in the provinces changed little, many wealthy provincials adopted Roman ways. They went to the games and some even wore togas. Within these territories, people were free to worship their own gods, as long as they did not offend the protecting gods of the Roman state. Every town had temples to the Roman gods, but there were also many other religious cults. One of the most popular cults was devoted to the Persian sun-god, Mithras. His followers met in secret underground temples to carry out their ceremonies, during which they sacrificed bulls and entered a trance-like state.

ROME ABROAD
Roman-style buildings appeared all over the empire. The Theatre of Orange in southern France is one of the finest Roman buildings north of the Alps. The curving rows of seats could hold 9,000 spectators.

ARMY LIFE
The province of Britain had a large army presence, and soldiers played dice games to pass the time. This cup and dice were found at a Roman site in London.

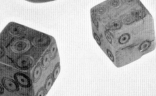

TRADING VESSELS
Roman merchant ships had deep, broad bellies, which allowed them to hold large cargoes. They were powered by two square sails, which could only be used when there was a following wind.

SPICY TASTES
The eastern provinces exported exotic spices across the empire. Pepper was the most commonly used spice, but the Romans also kept cardamon, cloves, saffron and coriander in their spice chests.

The empire depended on military might to defend itself, but it thrived upon trade and commerce. The army used up huge quantities of essential materials such as leather and metal for armour and weapons. In Britain alone, 12,000 calves were slaughtered each year simply to provide hides to make the soldiers' tents. All across the frontiers of the empire, small trading villages grew up to supply the army, spreading wealth throughout the area.

Trade went on across the length and breadth of the Roman world. Goods, such as fish pickle and olive oil, were sent all over the empire, packed into pottery jars called *amphorae*. Linen made in Spain found its way to the east, while glassware from Syria was shipped to Britain. Incense came from Arabia, amber from the Baltic. It was a world economy. Trading routes even stretched as far as India and China to satisfy the Romans' craving for

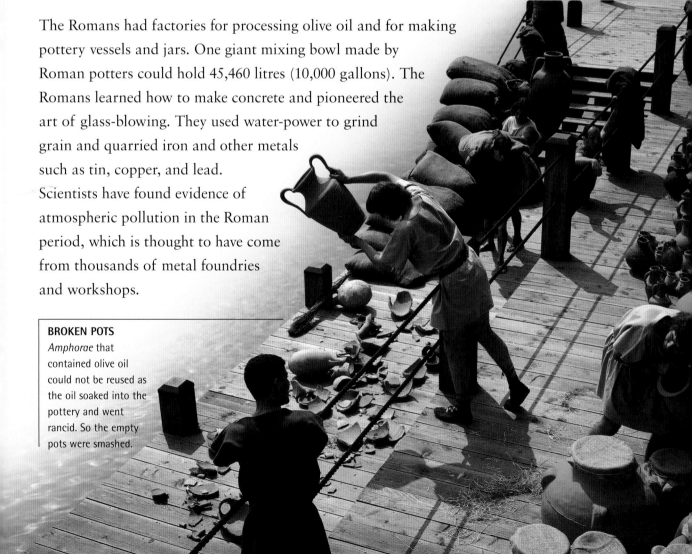

luxuries such as silks, spices and perfumes. Camel trains carried goods from India or China to coastal ports, where huge merchant ships were waiting for their exotic cargoes.

Nearly all of this trade went to Rome itself. The merchant ships docked at the wharfs at Ostia, the city's port, and teams of boatmen unloaded their cargoes straight into vast warehouses. Goods were then towed up the River Tiber by barge and were distributed to factories, wholesalers and shops throughout the city. Goldsmiths and shoemakers, rope-makers and metalworkers, carpenters and embroiderers all depended on the complex network of trade.

The Romans had factories for processing olive oil and for making pottery vessels and jars. One giant mixing bowl made by Roman potters could hold 45,460 litres (10,000 gallons). The Romans learned how to make concrete and pioneered the art of glass-blowing. They used water-power to grind grain and quarried iron and other metals such as tin, copper, and lead. Scientists have found evidence of atmospheric pollution in the Roman period, which is thought to have come from thousands of metal foundries and workshops.

IVORY
The Romans used ivory for decoration in furniture and jewellery. Traders shipped ivory from central Africa, via the Red Sea. Live elephants were also imported to perform in the arena.

BROKEN POTS
Amphorae that contained olive oil could not be reused as the oil soaked into the pottery and went rancid. So the empty pots were smashed.

A camber (curved surface) drained off rainwater.

The surveyor used an instrument called a groma to check the road was straight.

Building a road

Roman soldiers built most of the vast network of roads to enable the army to move quickly around the empire. Merchants later used these roads to transport goods from town to town. First, the road-builders dug a large trench in the ground. They put kerb-stones on either side then filled the trench with layers of stones, gravel and sand. On the top of main roads, they laid large paving stones. At each side were parallel drainage ditches, to prevent the city from getting waterlogged.

But the first and greatest industry of the Roman empire was agriculture. In the hotter, drier parts of the empire, grapes and olives were the principal crops, together with cereals such as wheat, oats and barley. Farm animals such as sheep, pigs, goats and cattle provided meat, milk, cheese and wool. In the early days of the Republic, farmers lived and worked on their own land, eking out a modest living. Later, much of the land was divided into great estates, owned by wealthy Romans. These huge estates were generally self-sufficient – they produced their own food and wine and had their own bakeries and bathhouses. The day-to-day running of the estate was the job of the farm manager who was in charge of a large staff of slaves.

HARVEST TIME
Iron sickles were used for the back-breaking work of harvesting wheat. Farm slaves did much of the heavy labour on the land.

For many slaves working on large agricultural estates, life was a short and bleak affair. Many were forced to work in

chains and had to wear iron collars like dogs, with the name of their master inscribed upon them. Slaves had no legal rights – they were owned by Romans who put them to work in their homes and fields. The most unfortunate slaves worked in the mines, where they had to crawl down underground tunnels to dig out precious metals. The average life expectancy of a slave has been estimated at 21 years.

The treatment of slaves was harshest in the years of the Republic, when there were a number of slave revolts like the one led by Spartacus. It grew more humane over the period of the empire. The Romans were well known for their readiness to free slaves and even to make them citizens. Roman citizens often arranged in their wills to free their slaves after their death. Many slaves could read and write, and some eventually became farm managers or trusted business assistants to their masters. Once freed, educated slaves might work as doctors or school-teachers, and their children automatically became full Roman citizens.

The supply of slaves slowed down as Rome ceased to conquer new territories and take prisoners of war. By the end of the empire, free men were doing much of the labour once carried out by slaves. Roman society was becoming mixed in every sense. There is a story of a Roman senator who was blamed for treating his slaves cruelly – he had forgotten, his critics said, that his own father had once been a slave.

HOME HELP
Wealthy Roman households had dozens of slaves to cook, clean and wait on their owners. Many slaves were well educated and artistic. They could be freed by their masters or save up to buy their freedom.

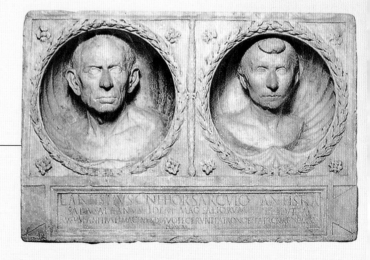

REMEMBERED WITH THANKS
The inscription on this marble tomb-relief records that two freed slaves, Rufus and Anthus, erected it in honour of their former master and mistress. Their mistress had once been a slave herself. Known as freedmen, they were not full citizens but had more rights than normal slaves.

CHAPTER TEN

The end of the empire

For more than two centuries, the Roman empire had enjoyed peace and stability, but by the mid-2nd century CE, it was showing signs of weakness. The death of Marcus Aurelius marked the beginning of a period of civil war and economic crisis.

MARCUS AURELIUS HAD LEFT the empire in good shape. Its finances were sound, and its armies had the provinces under control. When his son, Commodus, succeeded him in 180 CE, the omens for the new reign looked promising. Commodus was the first son to follow his father as emperor since Domitian 80 years previously. The "five good emperors" had all been chosen at an age when their characters were already known. But Marcus Aurelius believed that you could raise an ideal ruler from childhood. Commodus had been prepared for the role from the age of five. He was only 18 when he came to power and was hailed as the "most noble of all the emperors". Unfortunately, Marcus Aurelius was proved disastrously wrong. Commodus paid very little attention to his duties and left the business of government to his friends, who

◀ A carving from the Arch of Septimius Severus, Rome

LION SLAYER
Commodus identified himself with the semi-divine Hercules, the warrior and lion-slayer of Greek legend. He is shown in this statue wearing Hercules' lionskin cloak and carrying his great club.

were often guilty of bribery and corruption. He became addicted to the public games and squandered huge sums of money on chariot races. Commodus was jealous of the gladiators and had many executed for the sole reason that they excelled at their sport. During the public games in 192 CE, he decided to exhibit his own skills in the arena. It is said that Commodus killed 100 bears with javelins and cut off the heads of ostriches with such speed that they continued to run around him with their necks still bleeding. Outside the arena, he had many senators and distinguished Romans executed on the most absurd charges. His excesses became so serious that his assassination was almost inevitable. He was given wine laced with poison and, when that failed to kill him, he was strangled in his bed.

His successor, Pertinax was the son of a former slave. He had risen through the ranks to become governor of several Roman provinces. His attempts to enforce stricter discipline within the Praetorian Guard led to his murder after only three months as emperor. The Praetorian Guard then took the unusual step of offering the job of emperor to the highest bidder. The winner of the auction, a wealthy senator called Didius Julianus, ruled for 66 days before he too was murdered.

The empire was now plunged into civil war. After the death of Pertinax, three provincial governors had each been proclaimed emperor by their troops. Septimius Severus, governor of Upper Pannonia (in present-day Hungary) arrived first in Rome and declared himself emperor. He proceeded to defeat both his rivals in battle and ruled for an uninterrupted 15 years. It was an omen for the future. From this time forward, Rome would be ruled by military emperors who held power by force of arms.

Septimius Severus was a provincial, born at Lepcis Magna in North Africa. He was an efficient emperor, who improved the security of the frontiers and repaired the major roads. During his reign, he fought a successful war against the Persians and captured their capital of Ctesiphon. In 208 CE, Septimius Severus arrived in Britain on an expedition to subdue the troublesome barbarians living north of Hadrian's Wall. He was already 63 years old and ill, but he spent three years in Britain with his family and died at York in 211 CE.

During his reign, Severus had raised the pay of the legionary soldiers for the first time since 84 CE. He also permitted ordinary soldiers to marry. The army was the

SEVERUS THE BUILDER
This ornate column is from the Severan Basilica in Lepcis Magna and was built by Severus after he became emperor. His most famous monument is the triumphal arch at the Forum in Rome.

OSTRICH KILLER
This mosaic shows an ostrich being captured for the Roman arena. Thousands of animals were taken to Rome for animal hunts. Many were transported by ship from Egypt and North Africa.

The Roman army

The organization of the Roman army had changed little for more than 200 years. Soldiers fought in line about 1.2 m (4 ft) apart. They attacked with swords and javelins and protected themselves with shields. As the men in the front row fell, soldiers from behind stepped into their places. Any company that ran away was decimated – every tenth man was taken out and beaten to death with wooden clubs. At the end of their service (20–25 years), soldiers were given money or a plot of land to farm. As well as fighting, soldiers built bridges, buildings and roads across the empire.

A soldier carried everything he needed to fight and build camp in his backpack.

Soldier

The standard-bearer, or signifier, carried the emblem of a century. He wore a wolfskin over his helmet.

Standard-bearer

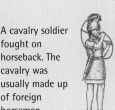

A cavalry soldier fought on horseback. The cavalry was usually made up of foreign horsemen.

Cavalry soldier

The trumpeteer, or *cornicen*, blew his long curved horn to signal each new command during a battle.

Trumpeteer

A centurion commanded a century.

Centurion

A century was made up of ten *contubernia* (80 men).

Century

A tribune was a staff officer who helped the legate.

Tribune

A cohort was usually made up of six centuries (480 men).

Cohort

A legate was the commanding officer of a legion.

Legate

Organization
During the years of the empire, soldiers were grouped into legions – units of about 5,000 men. Each legion was divided into centuries of about 80 men. The centuries themselves were broken down into *contubernia*, groups of eight men. The men in each *contubernium* shared a tent and ate meals together.

The legion
A legion consisted of ten cohorts. A cohort was a group of centuries. The first cohort, *prima cohors*, was bigger than the rest, consisting of ten centuries. The other nine cohorts had six centuries each. Every legion carried a silver eagle standard, which was a symbol of its power.

biggest single employer and the biggest single drain on Roman resources. Money raised by taxing the provinces helped to pay the soldiers' salaries. The days when the armies were made up entirely of Roman citizens were long gone. Most legionaries were provincials, who came from the areas where they were stationed.

It could be said that Roman soldiers typified the main characteristics of the Romans themselves. They were efficient and practical, dogged and determined, with a gift for organization that was the marvel of the world. They learned from both the victories of their enemies and from their own mistakes. More importantly, they had the power to create and destroy emperors. War on the frontiers was now almost constant as the barbarian threat grew more pressing, and emperors had to be good soldiers above all else. If they failed to win victories, or if they lost the support of their troops, they would not remain in power for long.

On Septimius Severus's death, his two sons agreed to share power between them. This arrangement collapsed when Caracalla, the elder by one year, murdered his brother Geta after ten months. He then launched a campaign of terror against his brother's supporters, and 20,000 citizens were executed or murdered on Caracalla's orders. It was not a good start to his reign. Caracalla's real name was Marcus Aurelius Antoninus, but he went under the name of Caracalla because of the kind of hooded coat he wore. Like his father, he was the soldiers' emperor. He raised army salaries once more and gave generously to veterans. His reign was marked by almost constant warfare, and his reputation was one of cruelty and violence.

HEAVY LOADS
Roman soldiers were called Marius's mules on account of their heavy backpacks. Each pack weighed more than 40 kg (90 lb) and carried rations, clothes and tools for digging ditches.

VINDOLANDA LETTERS
At the fort of Vindolanda in Britain, archaeologists discovered more than 1,000 letters written by Roman soldiers and civilians on thin wooden tablets. They included shopping lists and birthday invitations.

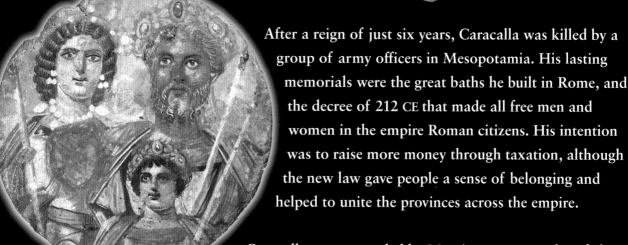

After a reign of just six years, Caracalla was killed by a group of army officers in Mesopotamia. His lasting memorials were the great baths he built in Rome, and the decree of 212 CE that made all free men and women in the empire Roman citizens. His intention was to raise more money through taxation, although the new law gave people a sense of belonging and helped to unite the provinces across the empire.

IMPERIAL FAMILY
This family portrait shows Septimius Severus with his wife and sons Caracalla and Geta. After Caracalla murdered his brother, he ordered that Geta's name and image be erased everywhere.

Caracalla was succeeded by Macrinus, commander of the Praetorian Guard. He was murdered after a year when he made the mistake of cutting army pay. Macrinus was followed by one of most outrageous of all Roman emperors, the 14-year-old Elagabalus. Through his mother's family, Elagabalus was the hereditary high-priest of the Syrian sun-god Elagabal. He built a great temple of the sun in Rome and devoted himself to the worship of Elagabal at the expense of public business. He married five times in three years, and frequently displayed his talents as a singer and as a dancer. He also took part in the chariot races at the Circus Maximus. It is said that he once gave a party in which so many roses were showered on the guests that some of them suffocated. While he paraded in public dressed in showy oriental costumes, he left the business of governing to his grandmother. The Romans were shocked by Elagabalus's behaviour, and he was eventually murdered by the soldiers of the Praetorian Guard in 222 CE. He had ruled for four years.

MONEY PURSE
Roman soldiers carried cash in leather or bronze purses. These gold pieces, more than four years' pay for a legionary, were found at a site in Britain.

He was succeeded by his cousin, Alexander Severus, who reigned for

13 years until he was murdered during an army riot in 235 CE. He was the last of the Severan emperors, the dynasty that had begun with Septimius Severus 40 years before. With the death of Alexander Severus, the empire plunged into chaos. During this turbulent period, known as the Anarchy, the empire was struck by plague and famine. Some 26 emperors ruled in the years between 235 CE and 284 CE. Most of these emperors came from the army, and all but one died a violent death, usually killed by their own troops.

Rome faced constant attacks on all its frontiers. The Goths, a powerful Germanic people, raided across the River Danube and defeated and killed the emperor Decius in battle. Another German tribe invaded northern Italy. At one of the lowest points in the empire's history, the emperor Valerian was captured while fighting the Persians and died in captivity abroad. The Persians stuffed his body with straw and displayed it in one of their temples. That same year, 260 CE, a general called Postumus, the governor of Lower Germany, set up a breakaway empire in the west (Gaul, Germany, Spain and Britain). It was an appalling and dangerous development that seemed likely to bring an end to the Roman empire itself.

After eight years, Postumus's uprising was crushed, and the empire survived. But the events of the 3rd century had far-reaching effects. Many cities, including Rome, erected new defensive walls. In Britain and northern Gaul, coastal defences,

ELAGABALUS
This bust shows the soft and immature face of Elagabalus. He liked to dress in women's clothes and frequently wore gowns encrusted with precious stones.

known as the Saxon Shore forts, were built to stop sea-raiders. The emperors were running out of money to pay their armies and were forced to devalue the coinage, causing prices to soar.

The situation was rescued by Diocletian, a general of outstanding energy and determination. He was a soldier, born in Dalmatia (modern Croatia), who was proclaimed emperor by his troops in 284 CE. He reigned for 20 years – longer than any emperor in the previous 150 years. Under his leadership, the defences of the empire were strengthened, and something of its past glory restored. Believing that the empire was too large for one man to rule, Diocletian split it in two, and appointed a general called Maximian as his co-emperor in 286 CE. A few years later he appointed two more junior colleagues, Galerius and Constantius. Under an arrangement known as the tetrarchy (rule of four), he divided the empire into four and gave each tetrarch his own area to rule. Diocletian took care of the eastern part of the empire. As a result, the city of Rome lost its central position in the empire, as each of the tetrarchs ruled from his own capital nearer the frontiers. Diocletian did not even visit Rome until the last year of his reign.

PHILIP THE ARAB
This coin bears the image of Philip the Arab, a Roman emperor from Syria. In 247 CE, he mounted spectacular games in the Colosseum to celebrate the 1,000th anniversary of the foundation of Rome.

RUINS OF PALMYRA
Palmyra was a rich city in Syria, with many fine Roman buildings. The ruins of its theatre are shown below. Its most famous inhabitant was the rebel queen Zenobia, who led a revolt against the Romans in the 3rd century CE.

Diocletian brought a new regal image to the role of emperor. He carefully stage-managed his public appearances, was addressed as "lord and god" and made any person coming into his presence kneel and kiss the hem of his robes. He revived the cults of the gods of the Roman state as a way of unifying the empire and insisted that anyone who refused to sacrifice to them should be dismissed from the army or government office. Because Christians would not make this sacrifice, he outlawed their religion in 303 CE, and started a wave of persecutions against them.

In 305 CE, Diocletian took the extraordinary step of giving up power, and retired to a splendid palace he had built for himself at Spalato (Split) on the coast of Croatia. He also persuaded Maximian to stand down. The two junior tetrarchs became co-emperors, and two

GOTHIC EAGLE
The Goths were split into two groups, the Visigoths (western Goths) and the Ostragoths (eastern Goths). Many Goths were skilled metalworkers who made brooches of gold inset with precious stones.

RULE OF FOUR
This carving shows the emperor Diocletian with his three co-rulers. The tetrarchs are shown gripping their swords and clasping each other's shoulders in a display of unity.

new colleagues were chosen to continue the tetrarchy. But this arrangement collapsed almost immediately, as rivals emerged to seek power. Once more civil war swept throughout the empire. The turmoil only ended when Constantine, known as Constantine the Great, became sole emperor in 324 CE.

Constantine is best known as the first Christian emperor. In 312 CE, he defeated his rival Maxentius for the control of Rome at the Battle of the Milvian Bridge. It is said that before going into battle, he saw a vision of the cross of Jesus in the sky, with the words "In this sign, conquer". From then on, he encouraged the spread of Christianity throughout the empire. He was the first Roman emperor to allow Christians to worship openly and he provided money to build new churches. But he himself was not baptized as a Christian until he was on his deathbed in 337 CE. With one exception, his successors were all Christian, and Christianity, for so long a persecuted sect, now became the state

RETIREMENT PALACE
This portico leads to the grand private apartments of the great palace Diocletian built for his retirement by the Adriatic Sea. He was buried in a splendid mausoleum in the palace.

they attacked Rome itself. The news was greeted with disbelief and horror throughout the Roman world. One great scholar, St Jerome, lamented that "in one city the whole world perished". There was worse to come.

VANDAL LORD
The Vandals admired the Romans and adopted many of their customs. This mosaic shows a Vandal lord on horseback wearing Roman-style dress.

TRIUMPHAL ARCH
Emperor Constantine built this arch in Rome in 315 CE, to celebrate his victory over Maxentius. Many of the reliefs and statues were taken from the monuments of previous emperors.

Civil war weakened the western empire, and barbarian groups poured across the frontiers into Gaul and Spain. As soon as one Germanic tribe had found a part of the empire to settle in, others followed. As the western empire fell into fragments, new Germanic kingdoms arose in Gaul, Spain and North Africa. In 455 CE, a tribe known as the Vandals, who had settled in North Africa, invaded Rome and left half the city in ruins. Barbarian generals took control of the army, and the western empire plunged into chaos. The end of the western empire finally came when its young emperor Romulus Augustulus was driven out of Italy in 475 CE by the Germanic general Odoacer.

religion. By the end of the century, pagan worship was outlawed throughout the empire.

Constantine believed that the empire should have two separate capitals. He restored Rome's position as capital of the west and built a magnificent new city on the site of the port of Byzantium at the entrance to the Black Sea. The new city, named Constantinople in his honour, was modelled on Rome, but it quickly became more important than its mother-city. It survives to this day as the Turkish city of Istanbul.

Ever since the 2nd century CE, the Romans had suffered constant attacks from Germanic tribes from the north. The Romans called these tribes "barbarians" and fought fiercely to prevent them from invading Roman territory. Constantine had created a number of small field armies that could move quickly to deal with attacks on the frontiers, but these armies were severely over-stretched. In the late 4th century, the Huns, fierce horse-riding warriors from Central Asia, burst into the region around the Black Sea and threw the Germanic tribes living there into panic. The Visigoths, a Germanic tribe from the west, asked the Romans for protection and were allowed to settle within the empire. But it was to prove a terrible mistake. In 378 CE, the Visigoths revolted and inflicted a devastating defeat on the eastern Roman army at the Battle of Adrianople, northwest of Constantinople.

Some years later, the Visigoths rebelled again under their leader Alaric, and twice invaded Italy. On the second occasion in 410 CE,

SAINTLY PAIR
This 11th-century mosaic from a monastery near Athens in Greece shows Constantine the Great with his mother St Helena. They are holding the cross on which Christ was said to have been crucified. Legend says that Helena discovered the cross on her travels in the Holy Land.

CHURCH FOUNDER
Constantine founded many churches, including the Church of the Holy Sepulchre on the supposed site of Jesus' tomb in Jerusalem.

CHAPTER NINE

The world of *the* Romans

At the height of its power, the Roman empire stretched from Britain in the north to Egypt in the south, and from Portugal in the west to the shores of the Black Sea in the east. It was the largest empire the world had ever known.

THE ROMANS DIVIDED THEIR vast empire into a number of provinces. These were lands that the Romans had conquered, and the people who lived there were known as provincials. Each province was ruled by a Roman governor, who was usually appointed for a fixed period of no more than three years. Imperial

provinces were ruled by governors appointed by the emperor, while senatorial provinces were run by governors appointed by the Senate. Ambitious young Roman aristocrats would hope for a succession of governorships, both senatorial and imperial, in the course of their careers. During the early Republic, governors were not paid, and some of them became corrupt, taking bribes and keeping money back from taxes. Later, during the reign of Emperor Augustus, governors were paid a salary, and officials were sent from Rome to check up on them.

◀ Statue of the Persian sun-god Mithras

While the western empire lay in ruins, the eastern empire (known today as the Byzantine empire) flourished for another thousand years. The emperors in Constantinople continued to call themselves Romans long after Greek replaced Latin as the official language of government. Although it grew steadily weaker and smaller, the Byzantine empire survived until 1453, when Constantinople was conquered by a Turkish army and became a Muslim city.

With the fall of the empire in the west, Europe entered a long period of decline. Learning and culture all but disappeared. But the memory of the Roman empire did not vanish. Roman customs, buildings and inventions continued to influence other cultures for many centuries. Today, many people still learn the Latin language, and countries all round the world base their laws and systems of government on Roman models. The lives of the Roman emperors have inspired writers and artists throughout history, and Roman roads, bridges and aqueducts have influenced builders and architects throughout the world. Millions of people flock to Rome each year to visit the magnificent temples, monuments and arches that still stand. Rome provided the foundation on which modern civilization is built, and its legacy

CHARLEMAGNE
This statue is of Charlemagne, king of the Franks. In the 8th century CE, he made himself ruler of western and central Europe and was crowned Holy Roman Emperor by the Pope.

Reference
section

◀ Neptune, king of the sea

Clues to the past

ALTHOUGH THE ROMAN EMPIRE CRUMBLED more than 1,500 years ago, its legacy is still with us. Much of what we know about ancient Rome comes from the variety of coins, buildings, documents, works of art, human remains and everyday objects that the Romans left behind. Over the centuries, archaeologists have discovered thousands of ancient Roman sites during building work or as a result of field walking, aerial photography or geophysical surveys (studies of the soil's structure). Excavated items from these sites give a valuable insight into the politics, history and daily life of ancient Rome, and help us piece together a picture of how the Romans lived.

BRITAIN

■ Londinium

GAUL

■ Narbo

■ Segovia

SPAIN

■ Tarraco

PORTUGAL

Rome

■ Carthago Nova

CORSICA

■ Cadiz

■ Carthage

AFRICA

Lepcis
Magna

Skeletons and teeth

Skeletons can tell us a lot about the health and lifestyle of the ancient Romans. The condition of bones and teeth can often provide details about what people ate and how they died. The size of the bones also helps to assess a person's age at death. This skeleton was discovered at the town of Herculaneum, which was buried under a layer of mud when Mount Vesuvius erupted in 79 CE. Experts studying the skeletons discovered that many of the inhabitants of Herculaneum had been suffering from lead poisoning, which could have been caused by lead cooking pots or water pipes.

Archaeological finds

Archaeologists have discovered thousands of Roman objects in countries as far apart as Britain and Egypt. These artefacts range from pots and pans to elaborate jewellery and vases. Documentation is crucial when artefacts are discovered. Archaeologists record the place and date the items were found. They also draw or photograph the artefacts to make a visual record.

Bronze
baking tin

Written records

Very few original Roman manuscripts survive, but, thanks to Christian monks who made copies of original Latin texts in medieval times, many writings are still accessible. Some examples of actual Roman writing have survived. This dog's identity tag gives the name and address of its owner. Other written records, such as poems and plays, letters and official records, give us valuable information about life in Rome. Buildings and statues are also useful sources of information as they often contain inscriptions recording details of important people or events.

Writers and thinkers

The Romans were prolific writers on a variety of subjects ranging from history and politics to architecture and mathematics. The first surviving prose work in Latin is *De Agri Cultura* – a book on farming by the writer and politician Cato (left).

Mosaics

The floors of Roman buildings were often richly decorated with mosaics, many capturing scenes of history and everyday life. Mosaics are greatly valued, not just for their beauty, but also for the information they provide. Unlike Roman paintings, mosaics – made from tiny cubes of stone, pottery, marble or glass – can last for thousands of years. Here, an archaeologist is using special tools to restore a mosaic featuring wild animals.

Black Sea

Constantinople

ASIA MINOR

Pompeii   Brindisi

Actium

Ephesus

CILY

Myra

CRETE

Mediterranean Sea

Cyrene

Alexandria

EGYPT

Finding evidence

During an excavation, experts known as environmental scientists make a study of the soil's structure and take samples of pollen grains or human or animal bones for carbon dating. Materials such as bone contain radioactive carbon that decays at a known rate. Scientists can measure how much of this carbon a bone sample contains and then estimate the age of the remains.

■ Extent of the Roman empire in the 2nd century BCE

Roman emperors

THE CIVIL WARS THAT FOLLOWED the death of Julius Caesar brought the period known as the Republic to an end. Octavian restored peace in 27 BCE and was proclaimed the first Roman emperor. Below is a list of many of the men who called themselves emperors of Rome. During certain periods, two or more men claimed the title of emperor at the same time. There were also periods in Rome's history when there was no clear emperor at all. After Diocletian divided the empire in 284 CE, there were usually separate emperors for the eastern and western empires.

Septimius Severus

68 CE

Galba 68–69
Otho 69
Vitellius 69
Vespasian 69–79
Titus 79–81
Domitian 81–96
Nerva 96–98
Trajan 98–117

Domitian

117 CE

Hadrian 117–138
Antoninus Pius 138–161

161 CE

Lucius Verus 161–169
Marcus Aurelius 161–180
Commodus 180–192
Pertinax 193
Didius Julianus 193
Septimius Severus 193–211
Pescennius Niger 193–194
Clodius Albinus 193–197

Marcus Aurelius

286 CE

Western empire

Maximian 286–305
Constantius I 305–306
Severus 306–307
Maximinian 307–308
Maxentius 307–312
Constantine I 307–324

Eastern empire

Diocletian 286–305
Galerius 305–311
Maximinus II 309–313
Licinius 308–324

324 CE

Constantine I 324–337
(sole emperor)

Constantine I

337 CE

Constantine II 337–340
Constans 337–350
Magnentius 350–353

Constantius II 337–361
(sole emperor after defeating Magnentius in 353)

361 CE

Julian 361–363
Jovian 363–364

Augustus

Caligula

31 BCE	**14** CE
Augustus 31 BCE–14 CE	Tiberius 14–37
	Caligula 37–41
	Claudius 41–54
	Nero 54–68

211 CE

Geta 211–212
Caracalla 211–217
Macrinus 217–218
Elagabalus 218–222
Severus Alexander 222–235
Maximinus I 235–238
Gordian I 238
Gordian II 238
Pupienus 238
Balbinus 238
Gordian III 238–244
Philip 244–249
Decius 249–251
Gallus 251–253

253 CE

Aemilian 253
Valerian 253–260
Gallienus 253–268
Claudius II Gothicus 268–270
Quintillus 269–270
Aurelian 270–275
Tacitus 275–276
Florian 276
Probus 276–282
Carus 282–283
Carinus 283–285
Numerian 283–284
Diocletian 284–305

Rebel leaders

Weak emperors led to the creation of rebel states. The kingdom of Palmyra in the east and the "Gallic empire" of Britain, Gaul and Spain were finally defeated by the emperor Aurelian.

Gallic rebel emperors
Postumus 262–269
Victorinus 269–271
Tetricus 271–274

Eastern state of Palmyra
Zenobia 266–272
(Joint ruler with her son Vaballathus)

KEY

Whole empire

Western empire

Eastern empire

364 CE

Valentinian I 364–375
Gratian 375–383
Valentinian II 375–392
Magnus Maximus 383–388
Theodosius I 388–392
Eugenius 392–394

Valens 364–378
Procopius 365–366
Theodosius I 379–395

394 CE

Theodosius I 394–395

395 CE

Honorius 395–423
Constantine III 407–411
Johannes 423–425
Valentinian III 425–455

Arcadius 395–408
Theodosius II 408–450

455 CE

Petronius Maximus 455
Avitus 455–456
Majorian 457–461
Libius Severus 461–467
Anthemius 467–472
Olybrius 472
Glycerius 473–474
Julius Nepos 474–480
Romulus Augustulus 475–476

Marcian 450–457
Leo I 457–474
Leo II 474
Zeno 474–491

Gods and goddesses

THE ANCIENT ROMANS WORSHIPPED dozens of different gods and goddesses, each responsible for a specific area of life or death. Some gods were adopted from the peoples conquered by the Romans, but most of the Roman gods were borrowed from the Greeks. Below is a list of the main Roman gods with their Greek counterparts, or other origin, given in brackets.

Aesculapius (Asclepius)
God of healing, who held a rod entwined by a serpent. Many sick Romans travelled to his shrines to pray for a cure.

Apollo (Apollo)
Patron of the arts and the god of the Sun and of healing and prophecy. He was the twin brother of Diana, goddess of the Moon and hunting.

Bacchus (Dionysus)
God of wine, spring and fertility, Bacchus led a life of wild indulgence and was accompanied by a band of merry revellers. He was often portrayed with vine leaves in his hair.

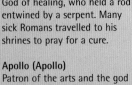

Ceres (Demeter)
Goddess of crops and harvests. She abandoned her duties to search for her daughter Proserpine who was kidnapped by Dis, god of the dead.

Cupid (Eros)
God of love. Anyone hit by one of his arrows fell in love.

Diana (Artemis)
Goddess of the Moon and hunting, her arrows brought plague and death, although her healing skills also protected women in childbirth.

Dis (Pluto)
God of the underworld, Dis was greatly feared. He rode in a black chariot and guarded the dead jealously.

Hercules (Heracles)
God of victory and business. He successfully performed 12 "impossible" labours.

Janus (Roman god)
God of doorways and bridges, he had two faces, one looking forwards and the other looking back.

Juno (Hera)
Goddess of women and marriage and queen of the gods.

Jupiter (Zeus)
Lord of the sky and weather and king of the gods. He married his sister Juno, although he was forever unfaithful to her.

Mars (Ares)
God of war and father of Romulus and Remus, founders of Rome. He was said to have a violent temper.

Mercury (Hermes)
Mischievous messenger of the gods and god of trade, seas and travellers. He wore wings on his sandals and hat.

Minerva (Athena)
Goddess of wisdom, crafts and war. Usually shown wearing armour, her symbols were the owl and the olive tree.

Mithras (Persian god)
God of the Sun. He was only worshipped by men and was especially popular with Roman soldiers.

Neptune (Poseidon)
God of the oceans and earthquakes, he rode in a white chariot and lived in an underwater palace. He is usually shown carrying his symbol, the three-pronged trident.

Proserpine (Persephone)
Goddess of the underworld who was kidnapped by Dis to be his wife.

Saturn (Cronos)
God of time and farming, his weapon was a scythe. He was said to be gloomy and stern.

Uranus (Uranos)
God of the sky and creator of all living things, he was married to mother earth.

Venus (Aphrodite)
Goddess of love and beauty and the daughter of Jupiter. Venus was said to have been born from sea foam. She was the patron goddess of Julius Caesar.

Vesta (Hestia)
Bright, gentle and pure, she was the goddess of the hearth and home. All Romans had a shrine to Vesta in their homes.

Vulcan (Hephaestus)
God of blacksmiths, volcanoes and fire. He was said to be lame.

Venus

Neptune

Minerva

Famous people

THE ROMANS LEFT BEHIND A RICH legacy in the areas of literature, history, politics, architecture and law. We still read the works of Roman historians, political leaders, writers and poets, and we still visit the buildings and monuments their architects designed. Listed below are some of the most famous and important people who helped to shape and preserve the Roman world.

Virgil

Boudicca
(died 60 CE) Queen of the Iceni tribe in Roman Britain, Boudicca led a revolt against Roman rule in 60 CE. When the revolt was crushed by Britain's governor, Boudicca killed herself with poison.

Catullus
(c.84–c.54 BCE) Poet who was one of the first Romans to adopt the forms and style of the Greek poets.

Cleopatra
(69–30 BCE) Cleopatra became Queen of Egypt in 51 BCE, and was a wise ruler, famed for her beauty, intelligence and charm. She was the mistress of Julius Caesar and later of Mark Antony.

Horace
(65–8 BCE) A poet and government clerk. His most famous works are the *Odes* – short poems about wine, food and nature.

Juvenal
(c.60–136 CE) A poet who wrote scathing attacks on Roman life in his poems called the *Satires*. It is thought that his poems led to his banishment from Rome.

Livy
(59 BCE–17 CE) A historian who also tutored Claudius (later emperor). Livy's vast history of Rome, entitled *Ab Urbe Condita*, consisted of 142 books, of which only 35 have survived.

Martial
(c.40–104 CE) Born in Spain, the poet Martial invented the epigram, a type of poem with a witty ending. His short poems describe everyday life in Rome.

Plautus
(c.254–184 BCE) A playwright who based his works on Greek comedies, although they include aspects of Roman life. He influenced later writers, including Shakespeare, who used Plautus's plots in some of his own plays.

Pliny the Younger
(c.61–112 CE) A writer and lawyer who exchanged letters with the historian Tacitus and Emperor Trajan, among others. His letters contain an eyewitness account of the eruption of Mount Vesuvius in 79 CE.

Seneca
(c.4 BCE–65 CE) A philosopher, poet and lawyer who was tutor and advisor to Emperor Nero. In 65 CE, he was accused of conspiring against Nero and was forced to commit suicide.

Suetonius
(c.70–130 CE) Historian, who wrote the *Lives of the Twelve Caesars*, an account of Roman rulers from Caesar to Domitian.

Tacitus
(c.56–118 CE) Historian whose works include *The Histories*, which give an account of the events of the Roman empire from 69–96 CE, and *The Annals*, which record the lives of the emperors from Tiberius to Nero.

Terence
(c.195–159 BCE) Poet and former slave, who wrote six plays adapted from Greek comedies.

Virgil
(70–19 BCE) A poet whose most famous poem – *the Aeneid* – tells of the history of Rome in 12 volumes.

Vitruvitus
(born c.70 BCE) An architect and engineer, who wrote a guide to architecture and construction called *De Architectura*. The ten-volume guide provided information on constructing different types of buildings and aspects of town planning.

Boudicca

Buildings

THROUGHOUT THE ROMAN world, builders and engineers constructed thousands of monuments, temples, bridges, theatres and aqueducts. Although many features of Roman architecture were inspired by the Greeks, the Romans also developed their own building styles and techniques. It was the Romans who invented concrete – a new material that was strong, light and easy to use. The Romans were such skilled engineers that many of their buildings of stone, brick, concrete and marble are still standing.

Arches

The Romans copied rounded arches from the Etruscans. Roman arches were built around a wooden frame that was removed once all the stones had been laid. The Romans used arches to build theatres and amphitheatres and to construct bridges, aqueducts and viaducts across wide valleys and rivers. The structure of the arch allowed it to support heavy weights over long distances.

Triumphal arches
The Romans built triumphal arches to celebrate victory in battle. These grand public monuments were faced with marble and were decorated with carvings of battles and historical events.

Theatres
The tiered seating in many Roman theatres was supported by arches. The Greeks built their theatres on natural slopes.

Amphitheatres
Tiered arches supported the rows of seating, which completely encircled the amphitheatre's central arena.

Columns

The Romans used five types of columns in their buildings. Doric columns are thick and fluted (having vertical grooves). The capitals (tops) of Doric columns are plain and undecorated. Ionic columns are more slender and elegant, and their capitals are decorated with twin spiral designs (volutes). Corinthian capitals are often elaborately decorated with acanthus leaves. Tuscan capitals are similar to Doric capitals, but their columns are plain, not fluted. Composite columns have capitals with four spiral motifs.

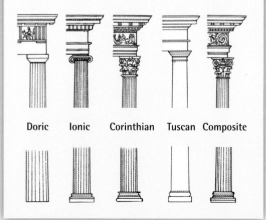

Doric   Ionic   Corinthian   Tuscan   Composite

Bridges
Arched bridges could stretch across rivers and valleys. The hills on either side acted as buttresses, or supports.

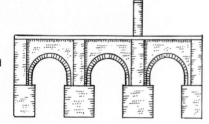

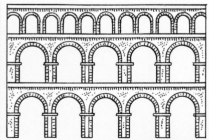

Aqueducts
Roman aqueducts delivered water from mountain springs to towns and cities. They consisted of a series of arches on several levels.

Domes

The Romans invented the dome when they rotated an arch in a circle and discovered that it created a strong three-dimensional shape. Domes are curved structures – they have no angles and no corners – and they span a wide space without the help of columns. The earliest domes were built of stone. But the invention of concrete in the 2nd century BCE meant that Roman architects could design much larger domed structures. Concrete was made up of rubble dropped into a sticky mortar made from lime (burnt chalk or limestone), *pozzolana* (volcanic ash) and water. The invention of concrete allowed Roman architects to design buildings with curved roofs for the first time.

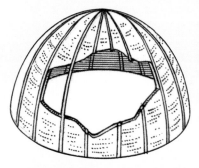

Construction of a dome
A domed roof is constructed by crossing a series of arches over each other, as this cross-section shows. The open areas between the arches were filled with wood, brick, stone or concrete and were often faced with marble.

Pantheon
The most impressive example of a dome, the Pantheon in Rome, was made possible because of the invention of concrete. It was cast with hollow panels to reduce the weight of the huge structure. There was a hole, called an *oculus*, at the top to let in light.

Vaults

Rounded arches were used to build high, curved roofs called vaults. These structures would have been difficult to build without the use of concrete. The Romans built vaults by placing a line of arches side by side to make a tunnel shape. Over time, the Romans learned how to construct a roof from a series of crossed vaults, which were supported by columns. This meant that they could make much larger rooms in their public baths and basilicas.

Barrel vaults
This tunnel-like structure was the original type used by the Romans.

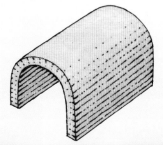

Groin vaults
A groin vault was built by crossing two barrel vaults at right-angles to each other.

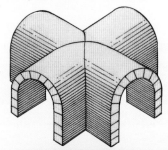

Glossary

Words in *italics* have their own entry in the glossary.

A

Aedile One of four government officers in charge of public buildings, markets, streets and games.

Amphitheatre A theatre with a central arena.

Amphora A narrow-necked, two-handled vessel, used for transporting and storing olive oil, wine or fish sauce.

Aqueduct An underground or raised channel, built to bring water into towns.

Arena The floor area of an *amphitheatre* or stadium.

Atrium The central room of a house, onto which most of the rooms opened.

Auxiliary Any soldier in the Roman army who was not a Roman *citizen*.

B

Barbarian A term the Romans gave to those who lived outside the *empire*.

Basilica A large public building, usually located in the *forum*, which housed law courts, offices and shops.

C

Censor A government official elected to keep a record of all Roman *citizens* and revise *Senate* membership. Two censors were chosen every five years.

Century A company in the Roman army consisting of 80 men, led by a centurion.

Circus A large racetrack where chariot races were held.

Citizen The status granted to free men (first, to those in Italy, later to all *provincials*) giving them privileges such as the right to vote.

Cohort

Cohort A unit in the Roman army. There were six *centuries* in a cohort.

Consul One of a pair of elected politicians who shared the highest position in the Roman government.

Contubernium The smallest army unit, consisting of eight soldiers.

D

Dictator A state official who was granted complete control by the *Senate* in times of crisis. He was supposed to rule for a maximum period of six months.

Domus A private family house.

E

Emperor The supreme ruler of all Roman territories.

Empire The period in Rome's history (c.27 BCE–476 CE) when Rome was ruled by *emperors*. The empire describes all the territories ruled by Rome.

Equites A wealthy social class descended from the first cavalry of the Roman army.

F

Forum An open area in a Roman town centre, used as a market place and for business.

Freedman A former *slave* who had been freed by his master.

G

Gladiator A specially trained fighter, named after his main weapon, the *gladius*. He fought in the *arena*.

Gladius A short sword used by a *gladiator* or a *legionary*.

Governor An official who ran a Roman *province*.

H

Hypocaust A central heating system, in which hot air created by a fire flowed through cavities under floors and in walls.

I

Insula A large block of apartments of mainly rented accommodation.

L

Lararium A shrine, found in every Roman home, dedicated to the worship of the household gods.

Lares The spirits who protected the Roman house.

Legate The commanding officer of a *legion*.

Legion The main division in the Roman army, consisting of ten *cohorts*.

Legionary A Roman *citizen* who served in the Roman army.

Ludi A term used to describe Roman entertainments, such as sporting events, games or theatre.

Lyre A harp-like musical instrument.

M

Mosaic A design or picture made with small pieces of stone, glass or tile, usually cemented in a wall or floor.

O

Orator A skilled public speaker.

P

Palla A shawl worn by Roman women.

Papyrus An Egyptian water reed that was pressed out to make paper and then used for important documents.

Plebeian A Roman *citizen* who was a member of the ordinary working class.

Praetor A high-ranking elected judge. Eight praetors were elected every year.

Praetorian Guard An elite division of highly paid soldiers, founded by the emperor Augustus. The Praetorian Guard protected the *emperor* and his family.

Procurator

Procurator An official in charge of looking after the finances in a *province*.

Province A region of the Roman *empire* outside Italy that was controlled by a Roman *governor*.

Provincial A person who lived in one of the *provinces* governed by the Romans, but outside Italy itself.

Pugio A dagger used by Roman soldiers.

Q

Quaestor A government official responsible for the state's finances.

R

Relief A carved or moulded picture that stands out from its background.

Republic A country whose rulers are elected by the people. Rome was a republic from c.509–27 BCE.

S

Senate An assembly of senior politicians who met to decide on affairs of the state, such as military matters.

Senator A member of the *Senate*.

Slave An individual without rights who was owned by another and used for various types of work.

Stola The main garment, or dress, worn by women.

T

Toga A garment made from a half-circle of cloth, which was draped around the body and worn on formal occasions.

Tribune (of the people) A government representative elected by the *plebeians* to protect their interests.

Triumph A victory parade.

V

Villa A well-off family's country house, often situated on a farming estate.

Index

Credits

The publisher would like to thank the following for their kind permission to reproduce their photographs:

Abbreviations key: t-top, b-bottom, r-right, l-left, c-centre, a-above, f-far

2 De Agostini Editore; 4-5 Getty Images/Robert Harding World Imagery; 6 Corbis/Archivo Iconografico, S.A. (l); DK Images/Capitoline Musem, Rome (r); 7 Corbis/Michelle Garrett (r); 8 DK Images/Capitoline Museum, Rome (b); 9 The Art Archive/Dagli Orti (t); 10-11 akg-images/Peter Connolly (b); 11 Corbis/Archivo Iconografico, S.A. (br); 12 Corbis/Araldo de Luca (t); 12-13 Ancient Art & Architecture Collection/Prisma (b); 14 DK Images/British Museum (b); Photo Scala, Florence/Museo Gregoriano Profano, Vatican (t); 15 Corbis/Michelle Garrett (b); 16 Corbis/Araldo de Luca (b); 17 www.bridgeman.co.uk/Musee de Tesse, Le Mans, France (b); 18 The Art Archive/Musee du Louvre, Paris/Dagli Orti; 20 Charlie Best (b); Corbis/Archivo Iconografico, S.A. (t); 21 Charlie Best; 22 Photo Scala, Florence/Museo Nazionale, Naples, Italy (t); 23 Photo Scala, Florence/Museo di Villa Giulia, Rome, Italy (t); 24 akg-images/Peter Connolly (t); DK Images/British Museum (c); 25 The Art Archive/Museum of Carthage/Dagli Orti (t); 27 The Art Archive/Museo Capitolino/Dagli Orti (t); 28 Ancient Art & Architecture Collection (c); 29 Corbis/Roger Wood (t); 30 Corbis/Ted Spiegel (l); 32 Corbis/Phil Schermeister (b); 33 Charlie Best (br); 34 The Art Archive/Museo della Civita Romana, Rome (t); 35 DK Images/Simon James; 36 Charlie Best (b); 36-37 Getty Images/The Image Bank/Alan R.Moller; 37 The Art Archive/Galleria Borghese, Rome (r); 38 DK Images/British Museum (b); The Art Archive/Antiquarium Castellama, Italy/Dagli Orti (b); 39 DK Images/British Museum (tl, tc); 40 www.bridgeman.co.uk/Musee Crozatier, Le Puy en Velay, France; 42 Charlie Best (br); www.bridgeman.co.uk/Musee d'Orsay, Paris (tc); Luisa Ricciarini Photoagency, Milan (l); 43 Corbis/Archivo Iconografico, S.A; 44 The Art Archive/Jan Vinchon Numismatist, Paris/Dagli Orti (tr); Topfoto.co.uk (b); 44-45 Corbis/Randy Faris; 45 Charlie Best (br, t); 46-47 Charlie Best (b); 48 akg-images/Peter Connolly (t); Charlie Best (b); 49 De Agostini Editore (bl); 50 Charlie Best (c); 51 Corbis/North Carolina Museum of Art (t); Getty Images/Taxi/Von Salomon (c); Topfoto.co.uk/The British Museum/HIP (b); 52 akg-images/Vatican Museums (l); 53 Alamy Images/MedioImages (l); 54-55 Charlie Best (b); 55 De Agostini Editore (cr); 56 The Art Archive/Dagli Orti (A) (c); 58 Luisa Ricciarini Photoagency, Milan (t); 58-59 Alamy Images/MedioImages; 59 The Art Archive/Musee du Louvre, Paris (br); 61 akg-images/Erich Lessing (tr); 62 Charlie Best (l); www.vroma.org (tr); 63 Charlie Best; 64 De Agostini Editore (tl); 65 Charlie Best (b); 66 De Agostini Editore; 67 Corbis/Sygma/Pizzoli Alberto (b); The Art Archive/Museo della Civita Romana, Rome/Dagli Orti (t); 68 Corbis/Roger Ressmeyer; De Agostini Editore (r); 71 Corbis/Dave Bartruff (b), Nathan Benn (t); 72 Corbis/Wolfgang Kaehler (t); 72-73 De Agostini Editore (b); 74 Corbis (l); 74-75 Charlie Best (b); 76 Corbis/Mimmo Jodice (b); 77 Corbis/Mimmo Jodice (b); 78 The Art Archive/Dagli Orti (A) (t); 78-79 Photo Scala, Florence/Museo della Civita Romana, Rome (b); 79 Photo Scala, Florence/Musei Capitolini, Rome (t); 80-81 Corbis/Vanni Archive; 82 Luisa Ricciarini Photoagency, Milan; 83 Corbis/Archivo Iconografico, S.A. (tl); 84-85 Corbis/Vanni Archive; 86-87 Corbis/Adam Woolfitt (b); 89 De Agostini Editore (bl); 90 Corbis/Sandro Vannini (l); 90-91 Charlie Best (b); 92 www.bridgeman.co.uk/Private Collection/Bonhams, London (l); 95 DK Images/British Museum (b); Luisa Ricciarini Photoagency, Milan (t); 96 Charlie Best (bl); DK Images/British Museum (tr); 97 DK Images/British Museum (tr, br); 98 Charlie Best (tr); 98-99 Réunion Des Musées Nationaux Agence Photographique/Le Louvre (b); 99 DK Images/British Museum (t); 100 Luisa Ricciarini Photoagency, Milan (t); 100-101 Charlie Best (bc); 101 Charlie Best (r); 102 Corbis/Roger Wood (b); DK Images/British Museum (t); 103 Ancient Art & Architecture Collection (b); 104 DK Images/British Museum (t); 105 www.bridgeman.co.uk/Alinari (t); DK Images/British Museum (cr); 106 Corbis/Gian Berto Vanni; 107 Charlie Best (b); DK Images/Lin Esposito (cr); 109 Corbis/Araldo de Luca (b); Index, Firenze/Alberti (t); 110 The British Museum (br); 112 Ancient Art & Architecture Collection (b); 113 Museum Of London (b); 114 DK Images/National Maritime Museum (t); 116 DK Images/British Museum (t); 117 Charlie Best (b); The British Museum (b); 119 The Art Archive/Dagli Orti (l); 120 Corbis/Araldo de Luca (bl); 121 Corbis/Francesco Venturi (bl); 123 DK Images/British Museum (b); 124 www.bridgeman.co.uk/Staatliche Museum, Berlin (tl); 125 Corbis/Araldo de Luca (b); 126-127 De Agostini Editore (b); 127 De Agostini Editore (tr); 128 Ancient Art & Architecture Collection/Prisma (b); The Art Archive/Dagli Orti (t); 129 Ancient Art & Architecture Collection (t); 130 Ancient Art & Architecture Collection (t); 132 Corbis/Carol Havens; 134 Corbis/Jonathan Blair (bl); 135 Corbis/Ricki Rosen (cr); The Art Archive/Archaeological Museum, Rabat/Dagli Orti (tr); Museum of London Archaeology Service (br); 136 De Agostini Editore (cr); 136-137 Index, Firenze/Alberti; 137 De Agostini Editore (tr); 139 Corbis/Roger Halls/Cordaly Photo Library Ltd (b), Roger Wood (t); 140-141 Getty Images/National Geographic.

All other images © Dorling Kindersley. For further information see: www.dkimages.com

Dorling Kindersley would also like to thank: Ben Hoare for editorial assistance; and Chris Bernstein for the index.